Fortress • 57

# The Great Wall of China 221 BC–AD 1644

Stephen Turnbull • Illustrated by Steve Noon

*Series editors* Marcus Cowper and Nikolai Bogdanovic

First published in 2007 by Osprey Publishing
Midland House, West Way, Botley, Oxford OX2 0PH, UK
443 Park Avenue South, New York, NY 10016, USA
E-mail: info@ospreypublishing.com



A CIP catalogue record for this book is available from the British Library

ISBN 978 1 84603 004 8

Page layout by: Ken Vail Graphic Design (kvgd.com)
Index by Alison Worthington
Typeset in Monotype Gill Sans and ITC Stone Serif
Maps by The Map Studio Ltd
Originated by United Graphics, Singapore
Printed in China through Bookbuilders

07 08 09 10 11 10 9 8 7 6 5 4 3 2 1

FOR A CATALOGUE OF ALL BOOKS PUBLISHED BY OSPREY MILITARY AND AVIATION PLEASE CONTACT:

NORTH AMERICA
Osprey Direct, c/o Random House Distribution Center, 400 Hahn Road, Westminster, MD 21157
E-mail: info@ospreydirect.com

ALL OTHER REGIONS
Osprey Direct UK, P.O. Box 140, Wellingborough, Northants, NN8 2FA, UK
E-mail: info@ospreydirect.co.uk

**www.ospreypublishing.com**

## Editor's note

Unless otherwise indicated, all the images in this book are the property of the author.

## Artist's note

Readers may care to note that the original paintings from which the colour plates in this book were prepared are available for private sale. All reproduction copyright whatsoever is retained by the Publishers. All enquiries should be addressed to:

Steve Noon
50 Colchester Avenue
Penylan
Cardiff
CF23 9BP
UK

The Publishers regret that they can enter into no correspondence upon this matter.

## The Fortress Study Group (FSG)

The object of the FSG is to advance the education of the public in the study of all aspects of fortifications and their armaments, especially works constructed to mount or resist artillery. The FSG holds an annual conference in September over a long weekend with visits and evening lectures, an annual tour abroad lasting about eight days, and an annual Members' Day.
The FSG journal *FORT* is published annually, and its newsletter *Casemate* is published three times a year. Membership is international. For further details, please contact:

The Secretary, c/o 6 Lanark Place, London W9 1BS, UK

## Author's dedication

To Jo Brayshaw.

## Preface

Out of all the monuments of military architecture in world history, the Great Wall of China is the best known but the least well understood. To stand high on one of its remote sections and see this great stone dragon twisting along the ridges both to the horizon behind and – so excitingly – to the distant horizon in front, is to experience a thrill that no other fortified structure on earth can provide. The Great Wall of China has been recognized for centuries as the largest fortified entity ever built, yet has remained poorly studied until comparatively recent times. It is therefore both impressive and elusive; presenting an appearance that can sometimes seem to be very simple and repetitive, yet at other times complex and baffling.

Even though its construction is well recorded, the mythology and political propaganda that has grown up around the Great Wall often tends to obscure any straightforward examination of either its historical record or the attendant archaeological evidence. From the myths of its unbroken construction history and unbroken length, and from the tales of human bodies being used to build it, to the notorious nonsense about it being visible from the Moon, the Great Wall of China is far more than just a defensive structure: it is a national icon. Once despised as a symbol of all that was wrong with China, the Great Wall now acts as a symbol of all that is right with it. Built from the dust of China and, in many places sadly, returning to it, the Great Wall has often been more pillaged than preserved and now faces greater threats to its continued existence than ever before. In today's commercial world, where the Great Wall's role has become one of attracting visitors to China instead of persuading them to stay away, a journey along its diverse ramparts easily reveals its vulnerability, but it also provokes more questions than it provides answers.

It is the purpose of this book to give a concise account of this magnificent yet daunting edifice based on the best and most reliable evidence available for its history, construction and usage. In this context I would like to thank Travelsphere Ltd, whose excellent tour of the Ming Great Wall provided my personal introduction to the subject. Professor Richard Merriman, with whom I walked several sections of the Great Wall, provided valuable insights into the geology of the Wall and its environment. I am also greatly indebted to William Lindesay, who probably knows more about this surprisingly fragile monument than almost anyone else on earth, and is doing so much to help preserve it so that future generations may be able to experience the greatest military wonder of the world.

# Contents

Introduction: raiding and trading 4

Chronology 8

Design and development 9
The Great Wall and its builders • The construction of the Great Wall
The structural and architectural features of the Great Wall

The Great Wall as a strategic defensive system 30
Mobile enemies and static defences • The Ming Great Wall – a ridge too far?

The Great Wall at the operational level 36
Defending the Great Wall • Signalling and intelligence gathering • Artillery on the Great Wall

The Great Wall from end to end 41

The living site 49
Life and death on the Great Wall • Guarding the Great Wall

Operational history 52
From boredom to battles • The Great Wall in modern warfare

Aftermath: the Great Wall as a symbol 58

The Great Wall today 59

Bibliography 63

Index 64

# Introduction: raiding and trading

The Great Wall of China owes its existence to the history of the interaction between the settled agricultural communities of China and their predominantly nomadic neighbours to the north. Nearly half of the territory that makes up modern China is desert, mountain or arid plateau, and for much of the country's history peoples whose culture and languages were very different from those of the ethnic Han Chinese occupied these lands. Some conducted agriculture on a small scale, but the vast majority lived lives that were sustained by what is known as pastoral nomadism. 'Pastoral' means that they herded vast flocks of domesticated animals, mainly sheep, across open grasslands, rather than confining them within corrals and feeding them hay. 'Nomadism' refers to the need to move around to seek renewed pasturelands while the ones they had just left were regenerating. The life of a nomad was a highly mobile one where skills at horsemanship were greatly prized. Children learned to ride at a very early age, and the whole experience of their lives acted as a training for future wars, when rapidly moving mobile units would raid settled communities or engage them in battle; highly skilled mounted archery was the nomads' greatest asset.

For 2,000 years the settled agricultural civilization of the Chinese Empire was regularly threatened, harassed, invaded and sometimes even conquered by these northern nomadic tribes, and the reasons why this happened provoked a debate that began centuries ago in the Chinese court and still continues in academic circles today. To the early emperors the nomads were just naturally warlike, uncivilized and even sub-human. The Xiongnu for example, according

The classic image of the Great Wall of China, as shown in this panorama of the Badaling section in 1987. (Photograph by Ian Clark)

The Great Wall at Shanhaiguan is an impressive fortress complex built round the famous First Pass Under Heaven: a huge gatehouse complex protected by a courtyard. On top of its wide battlements is a majestic gate-tower with a tiled double roof and colourful eaves. This view is from the west.

to a historian of the Han dynasty, had an inborn nature to go off plundering and marauding. Modern historians take a less prejudiced view, and several theories have been put forward to explain the rationale behind nomadic raiding. One approach is to consider the basic incompatibility between settled agriculture and nomadic herding. If the two activities could be carried out in separate areas then there was no possibility of conflict, but if by reason of drought or famine on their native steppes the nomads were forced to seek pastures elsewhere then friction would develop. In desperate times the nomads might even attack sedentary communities for food in order to survive. Unfortunately, not enough is known about the climatic history of the area to prove if this did actually happen.

Other historians have looked at what it was that the nomads actually needed from the Chinese other than food supplies in times of crisis, because certain goods and commodities could only be supplied with great difficulty within a nomadic lifestyle. These items included grain to supplement their diet, and textiles and metal objects such as weapons. There was also a need to trade luxury items to sustain the relationships between nomad rulers and their regional and local chieftains. Trade, in this context, meant more than a simple exchange of goods, and included such mechanisms as intermarriage of royal families, tribute missions and the setting up of border markets. There was also the factor of what the Chinese needed from the nomads. The Chinese heartlands were not suitable for the raising of horses, and cavalry was an essential item in warfare if the nomad armies were to be met on their own terms. When the Chinese were willing to allow such trade to take place, it can be argued, peaceful relationships prevailed. If for any reason these complex trade relations were cut off, and there were several instances in Chinese history when they were, then the nomads might take matters into their own hands.

One of the nomad warriors whose raids on China led to the Great Wall being built as one response to the threat they posed. Rapidly moving mobile units would raid settled communities or engage them in battle, where highly skilled mounted archery was the nomads' greatest asset.

In other words, the nomads needed either to trade or to raid, and when raiding was seen to be easier than trading, the boundaries between the two activities became blurred. Repeated and unchecked pillaging easily developed into control from a distance, as exemplified by the relations between the Xiongnu and the early Han dynasty. Control from a distance could develop into the occupation of patches of territory, so that the invading forces directed any economic exchange. The culmination of such a process was the conquest of China itself and the setting up of dynasties based on what were already quite sophisticated nomadic empires. This dramatic change happened remarkably frequently in Chinese history from the time of the Wei dynasty, who ruled much of northern China during the 5th and 6th centuries AD. The Kitan Liao dynasty (AD 916–1125) and the Jurchen Jin dynasty (1126–1234) had their origins in Manchuria, where their predominantly pastoral nomadic culture also included enough elements of settled agriculture to prepare them for the task of governing China through the use of taxation systems and the like. The Yuan dynasty (1279–1368) was established by Kublai Khan, grandson of Genghis Khan, who laid the foundations of the vast Mongol empire. The Yuan were overthrown by the native Chinese Ming dynasty, but the Ming were to lose control in 1644 to another northern conquest dynasty: the Qing (Manchu) dynasty, who ruled until 1912 and came from the same ethnic stock as the Jurchen Jin.

This long catalogue of failures by the Han Chinese to defend themselves against the nomads underlines why the control of their northern neighbours, whether by diplomatic or military means, became the chief preoccupation of successive emperors. It is also important to realize that the Chinese did not only have to deal with sporadic raids by loosely organized groups of nomads. The nomad threat was also expressed through several major campaigns conducted against their borders by the armies of well-organized steppe empires who already controlled developed economies. Their ambitions went much further than mere plunder.

The long-lasting threat from the north provided a considerable challenge that was constantly changing and developing. It was never one that could easily be met on purely military terms, because the direct approach of launching retaliatory campaigns into nomadic territory was dangerous and costly. The Han Emperor Wudi achieved some success in 119 BC when he mounted an expedition into the Xiongnu homelands, but there are few other similar examples. Improved weaponry for Chinese infantrymen to enable them to break the impact of a nomad charge was another possible counter-measure, but such small-scale tactics were only effective if the enemy horsemen allowed themselves to get near enough to the Chinese lines. Chinese cavalrymen were sometimes useful against the raiders, but they never attained the nomads' levels of skill at horsemanship. A more strategic approach was required, and a historian of the Song dynasty, Ouyang Xiu (1007–72), recommended the following way of dealing with the nomads:

> Our Chinese infantrymen are at their best in obstructing strategic passes, while the barbarian cavalrymen are at their best on the flatlands. Let us resolutely stand on guard [at the strategic passes] and not dash off in pursuit of them or strive to chase them off. If they come, we should close strategic passes so that they cannot enter; if they withdraw, we should close strategic passes so that they cannot return.

One fascinating aspect of the above quotation is of course the lack of reference to anything resembling a Great Wall even though, in popular belief, such a barrier designed specifically to keep the nomads out had been in existence for 1,200 years and had been continually repaired and maintained throughout that time. This is one of the great myths of the Great Wall, so that it is possible to read careless accounts of nomads 'raiding through the Great Wall', when no such structure actually existed in the specified location at the specified time. In fact the building of a physical barrier between the Chinese and the 'barbarians' was but one option among a range of policy choices that successive dynasties could exercise in response to their greatest preoccupation. Contrary to popular belief, it was an option exercised on very few occasions in Chinese history, but when it was put into operation it was carried out on a grand scale and, unlike military expeditions into nomad territories, it left behind a physical legacy. It is this physical legacy of impressive lengths of disparately constructed ramparts, built centuries apart with often little reference to each other, which we now call the 'Great Wall of China'.

# Chronology

| | |
|---|---|
| **221 BC** | Unification of China under the Qin Emperor |
| **215 BC** | Meng Tian ordered to build defences: the Qin Great Wall |
| **119 BC** | Han Wudi's expedition against the Xiongnu leads to Han Great Wall |
| **AD 550** | Rise of Northern Qi dynasty, who built some walls |
| **1211** | Mongols ride through the Juyongguan Pass |
| **1215** | Fall of Zhongdu (Beijing) to the Mongols |
| **1368** | Founding of the Ming dynasty |
| **1372** | Ming defeated by Mongol Army at Karakorum |
| | First military structure built at Jiayuguan |
| **1382** | Wall built at Shanhaiguan |
| **1429** | First use of term *chang cheng* in a Ming document |
| **1442** | Ramparts built in Liaodong |
| **1449** | Ming Emperor captured in the Tumu Incident |
| **1474** | Wall completed in Ordos area |
| **1482** | Mongol raiders defeated beside the Ordos wall |
| **1530** | Breech-loading cannon ordered for the Great Wall |
| **1539** | Building recorded at Badaling |
| **1540** | Rebuilding of Jiayuguan fortress |
| **1550** | Altan Khan attacks Beijing |
| **1567** | Qi Jiguang transferred from coastal defence to Great Wall construction |
| **1570** | Probable date of commencement of Jinshanling section |
| **1626** | The Great Wall is depicted on John Speed's map of China |
| **1644** | Manchus enter Beijing |
| **1677** | Qing Emperor decides not to restore the Great Wall |
| **1793** | Lord Macartney's mission describes the Great Wall |
| **1900** | Old Dragon's Head destroyed during Boxer Rebellion |
| **1933** | Japanese attack Shanhaiguan |
| **1937** | Japanese defeated at Pingxingguan |
| **1984** | Deng Xiaoping praises the Great Wall |

# Design and development

## The Great Wall and its builders

The first Chinese ruler to have exercised the policy option of building walls against the nomads is commonly believed to have been the first emperor of a unified China: Qin Shihuangdi, the tyrant who reigned from 246 to 210 BC and who is guarded in death by the famous army of terracotta warriors. Ying Zheng, as the Qin Emperor was known before his successful unification in 221 BC, was the ruler of the kingdom of Qin, one of a number of neighbouring states whose wars with one another gave their name to the 'Warring States Period' in Chinese history. Qin Shihuangdi certainly commanded the vast resources of wealth and manpower that would be needed for such an enterprise, but did he really build the first Great Wall?

The evidence for both claims: that the wall he built was the first of its kind in Chinese history and that it was in any sense 'greater' than any walls that had preceded it is remarkably poor. One characteristic of the military interaction between the warring states that the Qin conquered had been the erection of border walls between them, both as physical barriers to invasion and also as defining boundary markers. At least nine such walls are known. They were built between *c.*369 and 279 BC, and were of considerable length and manned by border guards. In addition to these walls the kingdoms of Qin, Zhao and Yan also built walls to provide protection against the nomads of the neighbouring steppes. Nor were these walls the first long barriers of any kind in Chinese history. References to similar enterprises go back as far as 656 BC.

It is now generally agreed that Qin Shihuangdi did not construct something that was completely original on the Chinese scene. Whatever it was that he built after his unification of China, it was firmly in the tradition that he himself had followed during the Warring States Period. The common acceptance is that he took the existing structures built by his rivals and augmented them to produce one great unified barrier in much the same way that he had produced one great unified empire. The process began after the Qin Emperor had successfully expelled the Xiongnu from the bend of the Yellow River in 215 BC. The key historical reference is found in *Shi Ji* ('the records of the grand historian'), the first systematic Chinese historical text:

> After Qin had unified the world, Meng Tian was sent to command a host of 300,000 ... and built a great wall, constructing its defiles and passes according to the configurations of the terrain. It started at Lintao, crossed the Yellow River, wound northwards touching Mount Yang and extended to Liaodong, reaching a distance of more than 10,000 *li.*

In several locations the slope was so steep that the final section of bricks that makes the parapet of the Great Wall was laid parallel to the slope of the mountain. This was done solely to save time, and even though the structure has survived for four centuries, it still presents an amazing sight. This wall at Jinshanling is a striking example, and the scale may be gathered from the people in the foreground.

In this brief passage we find the two key phrases that were to be re-used throughout history to describe Qin Shihuangdi's enterprise, as well as all the other walls that followed it. The first is *chang cheng* (long wall or great wall) and the other is *wan li* (10,000 *li*, one *li* being half a kilometre). Put the two phrases together, and Qin Shihuangdi is credited with building the first *wan li chang cheng,* an expression often used in modern Chinese literature for what is now commonly understood as the Great Wall of China. In this view, the Qin Emperor's wall provided both the prototype, the route and the actual foundations for what we see today, which is the result of later 'repairs' or the 'rebuilding' of Qin Shihuangdi's original.

Before considering the likely accuracy of this claim, we must put out of our minds any visual image of the mighty stone edifice near Beijing. That dates from the Ming dynasty (1368–1644), and any defences built by Meng Tian would have been much simpler constructions of beaten earth reinforced with wood. Another passage in the *Shi Ji* tells us how Meng Tian 'utilized the natural mountain barriers to establish the border defences, scooping out the valleys and constructing ramparts and building installations at other points where they were needed'. This implies a very sensible form of civil engineering. Meng's wall (or walls) augmented not only any surviving barriers from the Warring States Period, but also supplemented what nature herself had provided. This attitude had a long philosophical tradition behind it, because to the ancient Chinese rulers frontiers were the creation of Heaven, not of man, and the exercise of virtue by a wise ruler would bring uncultured peoples into submission. It was only when rude nomads refused to recognize such a profound concept that it was felt necessary to add to Heaven's gift.

On this basis one cannot envisage Meng Tian sending his 'great wall' sweeping unnecessarily along mountain ridges as the Ming were to do. It is therefore not unreasonable to conclude that, given the resources available to Qin Shihuangdi and his well-known ruthlessness in applying them, a *wan li chang cheng* could indeed have been built, particularly if one regards '*wan li*' as indicating 'very long' rather than a precise measure of distance. In fact over 1,000 years later in 1077 a certain Su Song was to write a poem at the strategic Gubeikou Pass noting that he was once again 'crossing the 10,000 *li* wall of the Qin emperor'. There may have been nothing left of the wall itself, but as a folk memory it still had the power to stir a poet's imagination as he passed through an area that had been a vital defensive concern for many centuries, and in which there had once been something very special, whatever it actually was.

In spite of all his enterprise and assets, the reign of Qin Shihuangdi was a short one, but his successors in the much longer-lived Han dynasty were to follow his example by placing some of their faith, at least, in the defences provided by long walls. Emperor Wudi's expedition against the Xiongnu in 119 BC represented a different approach, and when peace with the Xiongnu was proposed various arguments were put forward in favour of negotiations. It was pointed out that the other alternative to war – the erection of border defences – was not a good option because walls decayed without constant maintenance and therefore represented a long-term commitment. Yet even with this apparently half-hearted dedication to a *chang cheng* the Han emperors were to produce another version of the Great Wall. They did it by utilizing what remained of the Qin and Warring States' walls and adding extensions of their own. To

Meng Tian, the general commanded by the Qin Emperor Shihuangdi to built the *wan li chang cheng.* Meng Tian's resulting creation, even if not as extensive as is popularly believed, nevertheless provided a rich folk memory of the size of the wall and the suffering it caused.

The neatest brickwork is found on the upper surfaces of the Wall where the final 'skin' has a gentle camber and the joints are as watertight as possible. The highest grade of Ming wall was called 'horse road wall', and had pavements of carefully mortared and cambered brick or stone so that rainwater drained away to avoid erosion. Here the three layers of rammed infill, secondary brick and finished surface can be seen in a damaged section at Jinshanling.

some extent this was a natural process that arose out of their westward expansion along what was to become known as the Silk Road, but the new border defences relied on much more than just walls. A minister under the Wendi Emperor, who lived between 202 and 157 BC, recommended that the frontier area should be colonized with families resettled there to work the land, and as many as 50,000 or 60,000 men may have been involved in these *tuntian* (agricultural colonies). 'High walls and deep ditches' were to be built round them to hinder the Xiongnu's advances. We may understand most of these 'high walls' as small-scale defences for the settlers, but there is archaeological evidence that a long wall was built in addition, and that its watchtowers provided a link with the fortified villages.

The Han Great Wall undoubtedly contributed to the stability that characterized the mandate of Heaven that that dynasty enjoyed for four centuries. The Han were followed by 200 years of upheaval during the Three Kingdoms Period, whose civil wars, romanticized in Chinese historical mythology, found no place for long wall building. Towards the end of the 6th century AD the Northern Wei dynasty, who had originated in Mongolia, considered building a great wall to supplement the fortresses they had built against any other nomads who might be tempted to copy their example of limited conquest. But the plan was never put into operation, and out of the rival kingdoms of the time, it was only the Northern Qi dynasty (AD 550–77) who built walls.

With the reunification of China under the Sui dynasty (AD 581–618) the idea of a Great Wall was revived, but the three centuries of the rule of the Tang dynasty (AD 618–907) saw the borders of China extended beyond the lines in the sand that marked all previous 'great walls'. A combination of wise strategic alliances, good government and a strong military gave the Tang all the security they needed. A telling comment by Emperor Taizong that one of his generals was 'a better Great Wall than the ramparts built by the Sui emperor Yangdi' sums up neatly the attitude of the Tang to themselves and to their predecessors' military efforts.

In AD 906 the Kitans seized power in northern China and set up a secondary capital on the site of modern Beijing. Their Liao dynasty lasted until 1115, when they were displaced by the Manchurian Jurchens, who founded the Jin dynasty and made Beijing (then called Zhongdu) into their capital. But their control was by no means that of the whole of China. The Jin Empire lay to the north of the Yangzi River. From the south the ethnic Han Chinese Song dynasty fought the Jin for supremacy using the newly discovered weapon of

**The Han dynasty Great Wall with a detached signalling tower, c.100 BC**
Under the Han dynasty the Great Wall extended out into the Gobi Desert. It was made from rammed earth reinforced with twigs. Here we see a section of the wall with a detached signalling tower just behind it. The tower has been coated with clay that has dried to a brilliant yellow in the sun. The inside of the Great Wall has not been coated with clay and shows the layers of rough twigs and earth. A horse is tethered ready for a mounted messenger. There are two signalling beacons. The crew have raised one beacon to warn of the approach of nomad raiders, who are being monitored by crossbowmen on the Great Wall. The one on the tower is in action and black smoke from wolf dung is pouring out. The second lies ready. The inset picture shows the tower crew loading the signalling fire basket with wolf dung using chopsticks.

gunpowder. After 1126, when they lost Kaifeng to the Jin, they were known as the Southern Song and ruled from Hangzhou. But China was even more fragmented than this, because far away to the west the Tangut Xi Xia ruled. The celestial kingdom was ripe for invasion by a powerful army, and just such an entity lay not far beyond its borders in the shape of the Mongols.

The Jin emperor had long been concerned about the Mongol threat and had strengthened his north-western border with a line of fortifications connected by walls and ditches. But when Genghis Khan moved against them in 1211 this line, constructed far beyond the 'traditional route' of the Great Wall, proved to be hopelessly ineffective. The Mongols moved on two fronts separated sometimes by over 320km yet kept in constant communication with each other through highly mobile scouts. Genghis Khan took personal command of the eastern army that headed for the strategic Juyongguan, the pass that protected Zhongdu from the north-west.

Xu Da (1332–85) led some victorious operations against the Mongols, and was then charged by the Ming Emperor with building the defences that were to grow into the Great Wall. The first phase of construction contained no elements of linear defence. It was instead regionally based, involving the fortification of strategic mountain passes and the construction of individual towers in frontier areas.

Juyongguan is now the site of one of the most frequently visited stretches of the present Great Wall of China, but in 1211 there was nothing to stop the Mongol advance except some minor fortifications. The invaders descended into the plains around Beijing, where they plundered extensively but made no attempt to besiege the capital. In 1213 another Mongol incursion headed once again for Juyongguan, which the Jin had now reinforced with elite troops. According to some reports the gates were sealed with iron and the surrounding countryside for 50km around was scattered with iron caltrops. Still there was nothing resembling a Great Wall, but the Jin resistance was so firm that it forced the Mongols into a large detour to find another pass. More raids followed, one of which reached Fengzhou and gave the Mongols their first sight of the sea.

Even after the loss of Zhongdu in 1215 the Jin continued their long rivalry against the Southern Song until the Jin dynasty came to an end when their last emperor committed suicide in 1234. Looking northwards from behind their supposed barrier of the Yangzi River the Southern Song dynasty smirked as they contemplated the destruction of the northern upstarts who had once humiliated them, but as an ambassador from the Jin reminded them, they now had an even worse neighbour to fear. It was not long before the Southern Song discovered exactly what he meant, and in 1279 Kublai Khan eliminated the last remnants of the Song dynasty. China was united once again, under the first emperor of the Yuan (Mongol) dynasty.

The Han dynasty Great Wall with a detached signalling tower, c.100 BC

Stone drainage spouts were placed only on the inside of the walls so that vegetation growth, which would provide cover to raiders, was inhibited on the enemy side. This example is on the inner courtyard of the First Pass Under Heaven at Shanhaiguan.

A dynasty that was only two generations removed from a man who lived in a felt tent on the steppes, and whose descendants now controlled a vast empire that embraced Russia, Korea and Persia, was unlikely to show much interest in building a Great Wall. Their famous European visitor Marco Polo, who never missed a trick, makes no mention of one. But no wall, great or otherwise, would have prevented the Yuan from falling to the Han Chinese peasants' revolt that resulted in the founding of the Ming dynasty in 1368. The Mongols were driven back to the steppes from whence they had come, but from that moment on the stereotypical contrast between the 'settled' Ming and the 'barbarian nomad' Mongols meant very little, and relations between the new Chinese empire and the recently ousted one took a dramatically different turn. The Mongol conquest of China was a recent memory of a real event, not some hypothetical threat reinforced by sporadic raiding. There was every likelihood that the Mongols would return to try to restore their monarchy, so Ming deliberations about their border policies became matters of acute debate and crucial decision-making. Almost all the possible options – diplomacy, trade, military expeditions and border controls – were to be considered and put into operation in one way or another over the next 250 years.

The early days of the Ming ascendancy saw some victorious military campaigns against the Mongols under General Xu Da (1332–85). These campaigns were so successful that it looked as though the Ming might even conquer the Mongol heartlands, but in 1372 a Ming army suffered a crushing defeat at Karakorum, the ancient Mongol capital. The Ming reverse was blamed on extended supply lines and a failure to survive on the steppe grasslands where the Mongols were so much at home. Emperor Hongwu, the founder of the dynasty, began to think again. It was inevitable that the option of a physical barrier should be discussed, and of course it was more than merely discussed, because the end result can be seen today. The earth walls of the Warring States Period; the already legendary *wan li* long wall of Qin Shihuangdi; the frontier defence systems of the Han, the Sui and the Jin were to pass into folk memory beside the Ming dynasty's magnificent new creation: the Great Wall of China.

Like Rome, the Ming Great Wall was not built in a day and the brick and stone construction with which we are so familiar had to wait another century before even being started. The first phase of construction, which was placed under the supervision of Xu Da, contained no elements of linear defence. It was instead regionally based, involving the fortification of strategic mountain passes and the construction of individual towers in frontier areas. These towers were built close enough together to facilitate the sending of smoke signals. The messages thus relayed would then be conveyed by fast horses to the Ming capital at Nanjing: clear evidence that an offensive approach against the Mongols still had some life left in it. The second Ming emperor continued his father's work, but he also inexplicably pulled back several garrisons from the margins of the steppes, a poor strategic decision that would allow the Mongols to fill the vacuum thus created. Also, his late father's policy of placing loyal settlers around the border – all minor royalty in the Ming's case – almost resulted in the Ming dynasty dissolving into a civil war. But the Hongwu Emperor's fourth son gained a speedy victory and became the Yongle Emperor in 1402.

The new emperor quickly announced a surprising change of policy. The capital was to be moved from Nanjing to Beijing. To some it was a bold strategy that indicated a firm resistance against any Mongol challenge. To others the moving of the capital within a short distance from the unstable frontier was an act of madness. The Yongle Emperor, however, used diplomacy as well as military force against the Mongols, and achieved a certain stability until an imperial envoy was executed by the Mongols in 1409. For the next 14 years the emperor led successful expeditions across the border, but he was to learn, as his father had before him, that there was no possibility of the Ming conquering the steppes, and he died while returning from a disastrous war in 1423.

The Ming dynasty was like a rudderless ship adrift far from its natural safe harbour in the south. Thoughts turned again towards constructing a line of defence, and it is in 1429 that we first encounter the expression *chang cheng* in a Ming document. The effort began modestly. In order to protect settlers in Liaodong two stretches of rampart were constructed: one in 1442 and the other in 1447. Although they only consisted of rammed earth between stakes they represented the first planned wall system under the Ming and, as if to reinforce the need for such a barrier, the Mongols soon afterwards proceeded to inflict upon the Ming the greatest military disaster of their entire dynasty. The Mongol leader was Esen, who dreamed of restoring the Yuan dynasty and had managed to achieve the level of unity among his people that made such a thought possible. In the so-called Tumu Incident of 1449 the reigning Zhengtong Emperor led a Ming army in person to counter Esen's advance against Beijing. The Ming army was utterly defeated and the emperor was captured alive. The Ming had been humiliated for a third time in 100 years.

The ensuing panic in Beijing began to subside when it was learned that Esen was not about to press home his advantage. The captive emperor's younger brother was placed on the throne, and it soon became apparent that the Ming dynasty had now been placed completely on the defensive – permanently, as it was to turn out. Being unwilling to negotiate with the Mongols (and the new emperor's supporters were none too keen to see the old one freed) relations rapidly deteriorated. Again Esen failed to take advantage of the situation and died in 1455. A Mongol civil war ensued, during which the Ming steadfastly refused to trade with the Mongols and suffered raids as an inevitable consequence. The captured Zhengtong Emperor had been released in 1450, but on his return to

The walkways along the tops of the wall were often wide enough to allow five people to walk side by side. Where the slope is gentle the walkway slopes with it. This example is in Mutianyu, where loopholes may be also be noted.

Where the Great Wall gets steeper steps are introduced, and the steeper the sections the narrower the steps become, as shown here at Huangyaguan. Some flights of steps are so steep that it is useful to use one's hands as well as one's feet when ascending.

Beijing he was promptly locked up. Over the next few years, which culminated in the emperor's restoration in 1457 after a coup, a major programme of repairs to defensive works was undertaken.

By 1471 government opinion was moving decisively in favour of the building of a secure border wall between the Ming and their greatest enemies. The main initiative came from considerations of the security of settlers in the Ordos Desert region within the loop of the Yellow River. A fierce debate in government circles, conducted far from the reality of the area itself, concerned money. Walls were expensive, but so was war, so Yu Zijun, a pro-wall enthusiast, proposed that 50,000 local people should be relieved of tax obligations and set to work during the spring, a time when nomadic attacks on their homes were unlikely because the enemy horses would be recovering from the winter. An unexpected victory against the Mongols provided a window of opportunity and the wall-building project was completed in 1474. According to the official report, the wall was 1,700 *li* long and had 800 strongpoints, such as watchtowers, along its length. It had taken 40,000 men to build it over the space of several months. There were still some officials who remained sceptical about the project but, following an incident in 1482 when a group of raiding Mongols was trapped against the fortifications and cut to pieces, its supporters gleefully made the announcement that everyone was waiting for: walls worked!

Over the course of the following century more wall building was undertaken to capitalize upon the success of what had originally been seen as a stopgap measure. But the overall debate about the nature of Ming defence policy raged on for years. Sensible decision-making was hampered by political infighting, factionalism and a woeful lack of understanding both of the dynamics of steppe politics and the military capacity of their enemies. Up until the end of the 15th century the Ming had been very lucky that they had not had to face a strong unified leadership among the Mongols. But instead of exploiting Mongol rivalries to strengthen their own position the Ming took a ridiculously hard line of no trade and no negotiations, so the Mongols revived the old dictum of 'trade or raid'. Even more remarkably, the Mongols took advantage of the Ming's abandonment of the steppe margin by building their own defence line there. It wasn't exactly the 'Great Wall of Mongolia', but it served the same purpose as the forts the Ming had foolishly abandoned.

Being both unwilling to trade with the Mongols and unable to defeat them in battle, the Ming fell back on to the one policy option that was left. The Great Wall of China therefore came into being, not as a result of careful strategic considerations and long-term planning, but because nobody could think of anything else to do. The eventual result of all this vacillation, indecision and arrogance was the creation of the most amazing military structure ever seen in world history. By the end of the 16th century it was complete, but the cost had been enormous. The new use of brick and stone had multiplied the on-site labour requirements one hundredfold, let alone the higher levels of skill that were now needed. The most fascinating feature about this final phase of Ming military construction is that contemporary documents did not actually call their magnificent ramparts 'The Great Wall'. Instead of *chang cheng*, which had been used for the more modest walls of the 1440s, we read *jiu zhen* (the nine military regions or commands – two more were added when the capital moved north), which specified soldiers rather than the fortifications, or *bian cheng* (border walls). It is said that the term *chang cheng* was avoided because the idea of a Great Wall was so firmly associated with the hated Qin Emperor Shihuangdi and the horrors of its construction that lived on in folk-tales. Whatever the reason, it not only illustrates the persistent folk memory of the Qin creation, but also calls into question the popular notion that the Ming were in any way 'repairing' a Qin dynasty Great Wall.

Wu Sangui, the commander of Shanhaiguan, was the Ming general who allowed the Manchus to march through the Great Wall. In April 1644 the rebel leader Li Zicheng breached the defences of Beijing and overthrew the Ming dynasty. Just outside the Great Wall were the Manchu armies. The First Pass Under Heaven was opened to them, and they obligingly defeated Li Zicheng in battle. But they then rode on to occupy Beijing and proclaim the Qing dynasty.

One outstanding figure associated with the building of the Great Wall was Qi Jiguang (1528–88), a Ming general who had made his name fighting Japanese pirates off the south-east coast. Pirate raids and smuggling had developed partly because of the Ming's steadfast refusal to allow any of its citizens to go out to sea to trade with other peoples – an identical situation to the one that was causing such trouble on its land frontiers. So even though Qi Jiguang would now be building a wall rather than organizing a navy, he was already experienced at dealing with short-sighted government officials. On being transferred to the capital he applied his lively brain to this very different strategic problem, although the Ming government turned down many of his proposals because of their cost.

The construction and repair of the Great Wall continued throughout the time of the Ming dynasty, and was in progress in 1644 when the Manchus entered Beijing and proclaimed the Qing dynasty. The Manchu

Qi Jiguang (1528–88) was a Ming general who had made his name fighting Japanese pirates off the south-east coast, and was already experienced at dealing with short-sighted government officials when he was given the task of extending the Great Wall. The Ming government turned down many of his proposals because of their cost.

conquest was ironical in many ways. While the Ming had spent a century ignoring the Mongols, the Manchus, whose provincial base of Manchuria began just through the First Pass Under Heaven of the Great Wall at Shanhaiguan, had absorbed them into their growing empire. When the Manchu army entered China as conquerors they did not fight their way in through a bitterly defended Great Wall. Instead they marched through it with the permission of the Ming general Wu Sangui, who saw an alliance with them as a lesser evil than submission to the rebels that the Ming were unable to control alone.

The Manchu conquest doubled the size of China overnight, and its multi-ethnic empire provoked many changes, some of which had a direct bearing on the newly completed edifice through which the Manchus had passed with such impunity. Once the dust of conquest had settled the new dynasty had to decide what should be done with the brand new Great Wall of China. It did not mark a physical boundary – not that it had ever been intended to – nor could it provide a last line of border defence when the actual border was hundreds of kilometres further north. And it was certainly not a dividing line between civilization and barbarism now that the 'barbarians' were in control!

As to the Great Wall's future military usefulness, the major threat to the Qing was perceived as coming from the south via the maritime powers of Europe, so when the Kangxi Emperor responded in 1677 to a report recommending repairs to the Great Wall, his tone was decidedly negative. Repairs would be too expensive, and even if the Wall were to be restored it was too long to be garrisoned adequately. The removal of building material was nevertheless forbidden, but apart from this one positive note the long saga of building and repairing the Great Wall of China came to an end within only a few decades of its completion, and its long slow return to the dust of China began. Unloved and neglected, it lay across the mountains like a stricken dragon until it was 'discovered' twice: first by European visitors, and second by the Chinese themselves. It was to be temporarily stirred from its military slumbers during the 20th century, but apart

In most towers the room entered from the walkway is a gloomy cellar-like structure composed of interlocking brick arches, as in this example at Jinshanling.

Some bricks on the Great Wall were stamped with the name of their makers and can still be seen today. This example is on the Jinshanling section.

from this the part it played in Chinese life became that of a symbol whose meanings were constantly changing, a role that it has maintained to this day.

## The construction of the Great Wall

Whenever in Chinese history the decision to build a border defence was made, the style of construction of the resulting walls, forts or barriers would depend upon several factors. The elements of cost and military strategy have already been mentioned, and one other very important factor was the local availability of raw materials, because Chinese border walls were built in a number of different geographical environments. The nature of these environments is reflected in the different styles of wall that appeared in different places, and three general types of wall construction may be identified. They are:

1. Rammed earth reinforced with vegetable matter.
2. Dry stone walling.
3. Kiln-fired brick and stone walls bound together using mortar.

The first two types are associated with the early walls of the Warring States Period, the Qin and the Han. The third type only make an appearance during the Ming dynasty, where the two earlier forms are still represented in certain lower grade sections. Two other minor methods may be noted. The use of sun-dried mud bricks, which were weaker than rammed earth and more labour intensive, was so rare as to require only a brief mention, while the Jin dynasty walls were simple earthworks thrown up from excavated ditches.

In desert areas the soil was gravelly, requiring a large quantity of vegetable matter to bind it together, so layers were created by using piles of fine branches within a sturdy shuttering of horizontal wooden poles (usually of poplar wood) held together with pegs. The sandy gravel mixture was poured on top and rammed at the edges using hand tools. The whole layer would be compacted by men pounding away from above. In this section in the arid desert of Xinjiang we see the protruding branches that indicate the different layers.

Whatever different processes may have been involved – ramming, quarrying, dressing or bricklaying – every type of wall derived ultimately from its surrounding environment: either the stone of ancient Chinese mountains or the 'dust of China'. This latter raw material was loess, a windblown deposit found in great abundance and derived from glacial clays and outwash. It has accumulated over a vast area of China over the past 10,000 years since the last Ice Age. Loess can also have bits of shell in it from snails, and these can dissolve to form cement as calcium carbonate. Walls made from rammed loess were therefore self-cementing. The clay within it would respond well to ramming and also made loess ideal for brick making, both sun-baked and kiln-fired. The mixture of clay and silt in loess meant that it was easily moulded and had reasonable firing properties.

The most ancient form of walling in China was *hangtu* (rammed or tamped earth), whereby successive layers of loess were compacted within removable wooden shuttering much like that used to confine modern concrete while it sets. The 'yellow earth' was taken from at least 10cm below the surface to minimize the likelihood of including seeds or grasses within the mixture. The layers produced by ramming were about 20cm thick, and could be built up to 6m high. It was customary to dig a trench and use rubble stone without binding material as the foundations, and to spread a layer of thin bamboo between each section to facilitate the drying process. It was a method similar to that employed in making individual sun-baked bricks, and produced walls that were simple but strong.

Although this method, commonly used for city walls, produced some sections of the early defences, the environment of the border walls required some modifications. Careful study of the surviving sections of wall built by the Han dynasty out in the sandy Gobi Desert reveals an interesting variation on the rammed-earth wall. Here the 'reinforcement' was provided by red willow, tamarisk or reeds – hardy local plant life that could withstand the heat of summer and the intense cold of winter. The soil was also gravelly, requiring a larger quantity of vegetable matter to bind it together, so layers were created by using piles of fine branches within a sturdy shuttering of

ABOVE Where there were plentiful deposits of loose stone around it was sensible to use this material for wall building. A suitable stone, simply prised from the ground, could be arranged very effectively by an experienced dry stone waller, who would use small stones to lock the larger ones together and present as smooth a face as possible to the enemy. Properly done they could be very stable structures up to 6m high. This photograph is of a Han dynasty wall in Inner Mongolia.

RIGHT The most ancient form of walling in China was *hangtu* (rammed or tamped earth), whereby successive layers of loess were compacted within removable wooden shuttering much like that used to confine modern concrete while it sets. The layers produced by ramming were about 20cm thick, and could be built up to 6m high. Two workmen are shown here ramming the mixture down.

horizontal wooden poles (usually of poplar wood) held together with ropes and pegs. The sandy gravel mixture was poured on top and rammed at the edges using hand tools. The whole layer would be compacted just like the city walls by men pounding away from above. Finally, the frame would be removed and the whole surface coated with oily clay to provide a smooth face as it dried in the sun. This smooth face has disappeared over the centuries from the surviving examples so that the core of the wall with its layers of twigs can now be seen. In some cases the poplar framework was left in place to provide extra strength. If supplies were plentiful, the poles would not need to be re-used, and it is interesting to read descriptions from 1298 of local people pulling the wooden reinforcements from old sections of the wall where the inner core had been exposed by rain. The centuries-old wood was extremely hard and made excellent spear shafts.

Where there were plentiful deposits of loose stone around it was sensible to use this material for the work. The introduction of better quarrying tools enabled the production of rough-dressed stone blocks that could be used to build stone walls without mortar. Dressing was not always necessary. A suitable stone, simply prised from the ground, could be arranged very effectively by an experienced dry stone waller, who would use small stones to lock the larger ones together to present as smooth a face as possible to the enemy. Properly done the walls could be very stable structures up to 6m high, with beacon towers being built even higher.

The Ming dynasty allocated sufficient resources to wall building to utilize the natural environment on a grand scale and also to overcome the constraints to be found in any immediate locality. Stone was quarried near to the line of the wall and used to build a strong structure together with the kiln-fired bricks that provided the Ming's greatest contribution to the Great Wall landscape. The

ABOVE LEFT The mortar used to hold the bricks together was composed of lime, clay and rice flour. The addition of rice flour increased both the strength and the fusion properties of the mortar, and in some places on the wall the bricks have eroded faster than the mortar between them. Here we see bricks and mortar on a damaged parapet at Jinshanling.

ABOVE RIGHT Strong foundations for the Great Wall were very important, and in many places there was a layer of volcanic bedrock beneath the surface, which could provide a base, but this method does not appear to have been chosen automatically. Instead an artificial base was usually made from large dressed granite blocks. Here we see bedrock, stone and brick at a tower near Shanhaiguan.

How the Ming Great Wall was built – cross section through the wall and stages of construction c.1570.

**How the Ming Great Wall was built – cross section through the wall and stages of construction c.1570.** In this plate the successive stages of building the Ming Great Wall are shown in one composite section, although in reality each stage would be completed individually with sections between towers probably being the 'unit'. The stages are:

1. Levering the foundation stones into place.
2. Ramming down the infill as the stone walls grow.
3. Bricklaying using scaffolding.

bricks, which were about four times as large as a modern house brick, were produced by the thousand from numerous kilns, some of which still exist. In the firing process clay loses water and the silica starts to fuse with new chemical products. Dehydration is the most important factor in producing a good brick. In Ming China all this was brought to perfection by encasing the kiln in earth for insulation and firing its huge stack of bricks for seven days at temperatures of up to 1150 degrees Celsius. Some modern bricks are fired for only a few hours, and this old process produced bricks with considerable strength. Tests have shown that the bricks used in the Great Wall could withstand a stress of about 320 kilonewtons before fracturing – about the same as modern reinforced concrete. After firing the kiln was cooled by pouring water over it and its precious contents of bricks – characteristically blue because of the reduced oxygen firing – was carefully removed. Some bricks on the Great Wall were stamped with the name of their makers and can still be seen today.

A similar strength was also found in the mortar used to hold the bricks together. It was composed of lime, clay and a 'secret ingredient' – recently revealed to be rice flour. The addition of rice flour increased both the strength and the fusion properties of the mortar, and in some places on the wall the bricks have eroded faster than the mortar between them.

Stone blocks, bricks and mortar were combined to produce a unique and dramatic structure. There is a popular story about the self-confidence of the architect Yi Kaizhan, who calculated exactly how many bricks would be required to build the fortress of Jiayuguan and ordered that precise number. His master insisted he allow for some more 'just in case', so the architect ordered one more brick. That extra brick is proudly displayed in its unused condition on the fortress wall today!

A cross section of the Great Wall shows that it is wider at its base than at its top to give stability. Strong foundations were very important, and in many places there was a layer of volcanic bedrock beneath the surface that could provide a base, but this method does not appear to have been chosen automatically. Instead an artificial base was usually made from large dressed granite blocks

In most cases the first sections of the Great Wall consisted of dressed stone blocks cemented together around the core, which was filled as the height increased. At some point bricks would take over, as shown here in a section at Luowenyu.

LEFT The walkways are usually crenellated. At Badaling the crenellations are found only on the enemy side, while here at Mutianyu they are on both sides.

RIGHT Kiln-fired bricks were the Ming's greatest contribution to the Great Wall landscape. The bricks were produced by the thousand from numerous kilns, some of which still exist. The kiln was encased in earth for insulation, its huge stack of bricks fired for seven days at temperatures of up to 1150 degrees Celsius. This photograph is of a mock-up of a brick kiln in the Great Wall Museum at Shanhaiguan.

brought to the location, although some dressing may have been done on site. They may have been dovetailed for stability, and the inner blocks were tapered inwards to provide an irregular shape around which the infill could settle. The infill was a firm core of the local loess mixed with coarse sand, gravel and rubble. The rubble may have been blasted out using gunpowder or dug from ditches on the outer surface of the wall, which would add to the defences. It was firmly rammed to make it very strong and keep it stabilized.

In most cases the first metre or so of the Great Wall consisted of dressed stone blocks cemented together around the core, which was filled as the height increased. At some point bricks would take over, sometimes as an inner layer followed by an outer layer of bricks laid up to 14 courses high, which gave the wall its final appearance. Many sections of the Great Wall today show only the stone layer because the more easily transportable bricks have been removed for house building. It is where the bricks have either survived or been restored that the remarkable nature of the Great Wall is best appreciated. In many places the slopes up which the Ming bricklayers had to operate lay at 45 degrees. Part of the Simatai section presents a slope of 70 degrees at a height of 2,000m above sea level, and the resulting 'wall' is only 50cm wide with a sheer drop on each side. Ideally, bricks should be laid in horizontal sections making a series of triangular steps, but in several locations the final section of bricks that makes the parapet was laid parallel to the slope of the mountain. This was done solely to save time, and even though the structure has survived for four centuries it still presents an amazing sight for the uninitiated visitor.

The neatest brickwork is to be found on the upper surfaces of the Wall where the final 'skin' has a gentle camber and the joints are as watertight as possible. The highest grade of Ming wall was called 'horse road wall', and had pavements of carefully mortared brick or stone where rainwater drained away quickly to avoid erosion. With a low water table seepage upwards was no problem, and

Signalling and observation were also carried out from a large number of detached towers, most of which were on the 'friendly side' of the Great Wall. They could act as rallying points if the Wall was ever breached, but the primary function was to relay signals back from the Great Wall as quickly as possible. This example is at Huangyaguan.

rainwater gathering in traps was the main concern. The stone drainage spouts were placed only on the inside of the walls so that vegetation growth, which would provide cover to raiders, was inhibited on the enemy side. The walkways along the tops of the wall were often wide enough to allow five people to walk side by side. Where the slope is gentle the walkway slopes with it. As it gets steeper steps are introduced, and the steeper the sections the narrower the steps become. Some flights of steps are so steep that it is useful to use one's hands as well as one's feet when ascending.

The walkways are usually crenellated. At Badaling the crenellations are found only on the enemy side, while at Mutianyu they are on both sides. There are also loopholes for archery and gunfire, stone-dropping holes and in some places the curious *zhang qiang* (transverse walls) unique to the Great Wall that extended halfway across the walkway and provided defences against a sudden occupation of a section of the wall by a raiding party.

## The structural and architectural features of the Great Wall

The long stone and brick dragon that was the Ming Great Wall was interrupted along its length by numerous towers, gateways, water gates and forts, and was overlooked by hundreds of detached beacon towers. Spurs, some quite extensive, protruded from the wall at certain points and ran along neighbouring ridges.

The most common architectural features to be found along the wall are the towers, located at various distances apart from each other. Their functions may be summarized as observation, signalling, defence, shelter and storage. The main criterion for spacing the towers was the need to see any signals given from the next tower along, unimpeded by geographical formations. The particular vulnerability of the sector, the steepness of the slope between the towers and the location of minor peaks along a ridge could also influence the decision about where to build them.

Part of the Simatai section, shown here in a distant view, presents a slope of 70 degrees at a height of 2,000m above sea level, and the resulting 'wall' is only 50cm wide with a sheer drop on each side.

Spurs, some quite extensive, protruded from the wall at certain points and ran along neighbouring ridges, as in this excellent example at Huangyaguan.

The towers vary more in size than in overall function. Nearly all are square or rectangular, while round ones are highly unusual and may have been experimental designs. While the upper surface of the solid Wall served as the central floor of the tower, this was always extended outwards to give a larger space. The resulting tower platform was usually offset – on the inside of the Wall it could protrude for 5m and on the outside for about 1.5m. This would allow fire from crossbows or guns to be delivered from loopholes or windows along the surface of the Wall.

Many towers have survived intact or been very well restored. Others have lost their roof sections or upper floors, so that their inner structure can be accurately described. The larger towers had roughly square-shaped central rooms that could be used as a commander's headquarters, but in most towers the room entered from the walkway is a gloomy cellar-like structure composed of interlocking brick arches. Some were just this one storey with a flat roof and a parapet. Others had an upper storey with a pitched roof and battlements. The door lintels were of stone, and holes can clearly be seen where bolts and hinges were fitted for the wooden doors that once enclosed them.

The introduction of the more elaborate styles of towers to the Great Wall is credited to Qi Jiguang, whose report on existing sections of the Wall stated that the soldiers had no protection against heat or rain in summer or the sleet and snow of winter, while ammunition and weapons lay exposed to the weather. Some of the new ones, which housed between 30 and 50 men, incorporated the

**Cutaway reconstruction of a tower on the Ming Great Wall c.1570.**

The towers were very important components of the Ming Great Wall. This example is fairly typical. The upper surface of the solid Great Wall serves as the central floor of the tower, extended outwards to give a larger space. The resulting tower platform is offset to allow fire from crossbows or guns to be delivered from windows along the surface of the Wall. The roughly square-shaped central room could be used as a commander's headquarters. It is a gloomy cellar-like structure composed of interlocking brick arches. There is an upper storey with a pitched roof and battlements. Wooden doors are fitted. The entrance from the 'friendly side' gives access only on to the walkway.

**Cutaway reconstruction of a tower on the Ming Great Wall c.1570.**

The larger towers on the Great Wall, as here at Huangyaguan, had an upper storey and pitched roofs.

'luxury' of stone platforms to sleep on, heated by coal fires. The larger towers were like mini-castles that could withstand a siege. Some even had access only by means of retractable ladders, and as they were well stocked with weapons, ammunition, provisions and signalling materials their garrisons could hold out inside their towers for longer than any enemy might be expected to endure outside. Other towers were used primarily for storage, but all the towers shared one vital function: signalling, which will be described in a later section.

Signalling and observation was also carried out from a large number of detached towers, most of which were on the 'friendly side' of the Great Wall. They could act as rallying points if the Wall was ever breached, but the primary function was to relay signals back from the Great Wall as quickly as possible. By the end of the Ming dynasty there were literally thousands of them, and although most were not physically linked to the Great Wall by spurs they were an integral part of the 'defence in depth' that the entire system represented. Their value was nonetheless sometimes questioned. In 1554 the governor general of Datong expressed concern that if the Mongols attacked in force the crews of the nearby towers could not help in the defence of the Wall. If the Wall was then breached the crews would take flight and flee. He therefore proposed to build more towers across the Wall in 'enemy territory' – 20 or 30 paces away from the Wall and 300 paces apart. Funds were made available and some were actually built, but in 1574 we read that 'if observation towers are too far outside the border wall the crews feel isolated, and in the case of an attack they dare not shoot an arrow!'

The simplest entrances to the Great Wall did not allow access through it but only on to the walkway. These portals were open only on to the 'friendly' side, which led to a steep flight of steps on to the wall itself. Adjacent to the most massive gatehouses there was also a long slope leading directly on to the wall: a useful but vulnerable asset.

Because the Ming Great Wall was not in any sense China's 'border' the long barrier was never seen as the medieval equivalent of a totally impenetrable razor wire frontier. Instead there were certain places where the wall could be crossed.

Water, as well as people, had to pass through the Great Wall at certain places, and some elaborate water gates and bridges have survived; but the most elaborate examples of crossing places along the Great Wall were to be found within the strategic mountain passes, like Juyongguan or Gubeikou, that provided the main invasion routes for centuries. Here, in addition to the Great Wall, were multiple gates, extra fortifications, barracks and frequently complete towns with flourishing markets crammed into the narrow flat land of the pass from where the adjacent sections of the Great Wall soared off along the mountains on either side. These 'garrison towns' became important commercial centres.

The actual gates in the fortified passes were of course very tightly controlled. Typically they funnelled visitors into arched tunnels through the wall under a fortified gatehouse. More elaborate examples were multiple gateways, often turning through ninety degrees through a totally enclosed inner courtyard. Guards on the parapets above could monitor all traffic, and with the provision of strong wooden gates any unwelcome visitor could be trapped within the courtyard and subjected to murderous fire. Gateways like these became military hubs, and barracks, armouries and horse yards were built against the inner surface of the wall.

One outstanding example is the fortified gatehouse of Shanhaiguan that bears a notice dating from Ming times proclaiming that it is the 'First Pass Under Heaven'. On top of its wide battlements is a majestic gate-tower with a tiled double roof and colourful eaves. On its western side is a wide ramp giving access to the walkway, while on the eastern side is an enclosed courtyard. Travellers passing through go into a dark tunnel under the gatehouse itself, and then have to turn through 90 degrees to leave the courtyard. Two other towers lie very near to the great gatehouse. There is also a very large corner tower to the south that forms an angle with the town walls.

The more elaborate Jiayuguan, far away at the western extremity of the Ming Great Wall, presents the appearance of a fantastic medieval castle. An earth-walled fort was first built here in 1372. Additions were made in 1495 and 1506, and then the whole edifice was rebuilt around 1540. Its walls were nearly doubled in height, in some cases by adding brick courses to the existing rammed earth walls. The main castle is trapezoidal in shape measuring 650m in circumference. It has two gates. The eastern gate is called the Guanghuamen (Bright Gate) while the western one is the Royuanmen (Gate for Conciliation with Remote Peoples). Both gates are entered through narrow arched passages. On top of the actual gatehouses are some very imposing three-storey towers, while a similar structure lies just in front of the eastern gate at ground level. Each looks like a fantastic Chinese temple, colonnaded with pillars and with curved roofs. There are also wide access ramps on their northern sides and a tower at each of the four corners of the inner fortress and in the middle of both the north and south walls. The walls, embrasured on their outside faces, are 10.6m high, 5m thick at the bottom and 2m wide at the top. Outer walls of a lesser height encircle it on every side but the east, and on the west the passage through this outer wall makes an extra protective gateway on that more vulnerable side.

The Great Wall also relied on the walled towns and villages around it as part of the overall defensive system. The rural population lived mostly outside these towns, but at the approach of enemy raiders they were required to move inside for their protection. To a farmer this was easier said that done. It was difficult to abandon fields at short notice, whatever the strategic plan might have said.

A curved archway giving access to the Great Wall on the Jinshanling section. Note the use of stone as a foundation, and the survival of the carved block that once took the hinge for a door.

Barracks, armouries and horse yards were built against the inner surface of the Great Wall at passes. This restored example of a Ming barracks is at Huangyaguan and now houses a hotel.

# The Great Wall as a strategic defensive system

## Mobile enemies and static defences

In one sense it is not surprising that among the options exercised to control the nomads should be the building of walls, because in pre-modern China walls were everywhere. Hardly a village existed that did not have some form of wall round it, and a city without a wall was as inconceivable as a house without a roof. It is therefore perfectly understandable that a culture that so valued walls for the defence and delineation of its property should consider extending the principle beyond merely enclosing a village or a city to enclosing a section of territory, particularly when the nomads who represented the main threat to that territory depended upon unhindered mobility for their success.

The presentation of a static defence against a mobile enemy had some very sound reasoning behind it. The Mongols, who were the finest exponents of nomad warfare, worked on the principle of 'advance separately – attack united', and nearly always moved in widely separated columns. When faced by an enemy force or by a fortified town these columns could reunite at remarkable speed. The superior mobility of the Mongol army therefore provided them with security similar to that given by concentration to less mobile armies, and this was something that the existence of a linear barrier like the Great Wall could hinder.

One reason why the existence of linear barriers could provide a defence against the Mongols lies in the refutation of a very common myth about nomadic armies. Contrary to their popular image, nomad armies' movements were never conducted at a gallop except at the final moment of closing with an enemy. The Mongols may have had a highly mobile army, but the fighting troops were always followed by a huge and cumbersome support mechanism in the form of their families and flocks. The sheep were herded while the people

The larger towers had roughly square-shaped central rooms that could be used as a commander's headquarters, shown here in this ruined shell of a tower at Jinshanling.

The largest towers were like mini-castles that could withstand a siege. Some even had access only by means of retractable ladders, and were well stocked with weapons, ammunition, provisions and signalling materials. Other towers were used primarily for storage. This is the so-called Store Tower at Jinshanling, which was actually the commander's headquarters for the sector.

and their tents were transported on carts that moved very slowly compared to the rapid cavalry. The cavalrymen's horses also had to have sufficient time to graze from the grasslands that they passed through. As fodder is more compact than growing grass, grazing is a much longer process if the animal is to receive the same nutritional value. There was also the question of the large numbers of horses the Mongols took on campaign. This system allowed fast remounts in the battle situation, but all the horses had to be fed, and horses not being ridden would require only marginally less energy than the current mount. The enormous amount of grass that a Mongol army would consume meant that the army had to keep moving to yield fresh supplies. The system adopted by the Mongol armies was to move their animals in the morning, graze them during the afternoon and rest them by night. The Mongols' military movements were therefore not merely lightning-fast sweeps out of the sunset. That tactic was just the culmination of a longer and slower process, and the final charge against an army or a settlement was merely the death blow. During the Chinese campaign of 1216–17 the average daily march was only 23km.

The above considerations lay behind the decision by the Chinese to build a succession of barriers that broke up the pattern of the nomad armies' advances by directing them in ways that were most favourable to the defenders of that territory. It therefore allowed defending commanders to practise the sound military principle of economy of forces, but the building of the Great Wall, of course, was intended to do more than merely hinder the advance of an enemy army. It could also stall his progress completely by providing a genuine defensive barrier that he would either have to break down, besiege or abandon, and the experience in the Ordos during 1482 appeared to confirm this.

From the time of Genghis Khan's first campaigns onwards the Mongols had disliked walls. When they attacked the Xi Xia early in the 13th century the need to conduct sieges against fortified positions greatly hindered their progress until they acquired expertise in siege warfare from captured technicians. Even then, the time it took to mount catapults against a city wall or starve out a population was not to the liking of a mobile force. One way in which the Mongols speeded up the taking of cities was to use the psychological pressure that came from their reputation for wholesale slaughter. This could cause such fear in a population that the news of the Mongol advance meant that surrender of the next target on the Mongols' own terms was almost inevitable.

## The Ming Great Wall – a ridge too far?

The Ming Great Wall was therefore an extension of a sound principle that had served China for many centuries. In ancient China walled towns had been the empire's finest insurance policy, so the Ming dynasty applied this tried and tested method to a much larger defensible space. But it is difficult to link this common-sense approach to the decision to build the Great Wall across precipitous mountain ridges covered with vegetation and loose rocks where no army would think of crossing anyway. Furthermore, historical records show that all invasions or attempted invasions of Chinese territory began along the major routes that were often defined by mountain passes. The Mongol advance against Beijing in 1213 is a case in point. The pass of Juyongguan was fortified, its gates were sealed and caltrops were scattered. This comparatively simple solution alone persuaded the Mongols to make a very wide detour, even though the slopes up which the Great Wall of China was later to be built were then completely undefended! So why did the Ming go to such trouble and expense to fortify that which apparently never needed to be fortified? This is an interesting question that springs to one's mind when walking along the dramatic 'switchbacks' on, say, the Jinshanling section, where one feels that in such places the Great Wall exists only to defend its own existence.

The Ming Great Wall runs across precipitous mountain ridges covered with vegetation and loose rocks where no army would think of crossing, like this dramatic 'switchback' on the Jinshanling section, where one feels that in such places the Great Wall exists only to defend its own existence.

Several theories may be put forward to explain the presence of the Great Wall where common sense may suggest that it was not needed. One explanation sees the Ming Great Wall as more of a political creation than a military one. Resources were plentiful, so if certain sections demanded that a long wall should be built across mountains for sound military reasons, why not go the whole hog and join it all up? It gave work, prestige and a reassurance of security to the Chinese population that disjointed and isolated sections could not provide.

A further explanation may lie in the genuine usefulness of the towers along the Great Wall. Each was a little castle in its own right and provided observational, signalling and defensive functions that would be of real use in handling a nomad invasion. But for the towers to work effectively there had to be good communication links between them. This did not only concern signalling, but involved the provision of covering fire and the rapid movement of troops from one tower to another if they were needed. It was therefore logical to link the towers by an all-weather defensible walkway. On this model the 'stone dragon' is merely the means of linking the key defensive installations of the towers, so apart from them the magnificent overall structure is little more than the 'Great Footpath of China'!

Support for this theory is provided by the existence of spurs from the Great Wall to isolated towers, often at a considerable distance away, and by the observation of gaps in the Great Wall. By 'gaps' I do not mean large sections that were never completed, but small gaps where the Great Wall hits a 'dead end' at a very steep slope or even a sheer cliff face, such as the 'yellow cliff' at Huangyaguan. The Simatai sector may boast a wall that rises at an angle of 70 degrees, but the builders of the Great Wall were no fools. There were places where to build an easy link would prove to be as much to an attacker's advantage as it was to a defender's, so it was left as a rough scramble up a narrow mountain path, which could be defended more easily.

There is another way of looking at the Ming Great Wall, and that is as a deterrent. If we regard the provision of defences across the mountain passes as the key element of the Great Wall system, then we may see the addition of lines radiating from them up the hillsides in a slightly different light. The Gubeikou section is a very good example. The area through which the modern road travels is quite wide, and lengths of wall and towers seem to be all around. Climb but a short distance up, walk a little way along until the valley disappears from view, and the sight of the Great Wall apparently heading to infinity in both directions is one that provokes feelings of awe. If this can be done to the modern visitor, what might have been the effects on a hostile invader? Would not the sight have both intimidated him and reminded him of the vast military resources possessed by the land he was so presumptuously thinking of invading? Might he not have been persuaded, like 'Proud Edward' at the hands of the Scots, 'tae think again'?

The simplest entrances to the Great Wall did not allow access through it but only on to the walkway. These portals were open only on to the 'friendly' side, which led to a steep flight of steps on to the Wall itself. This example is at Mutianyu.

Yet there were occasions when the Great Wall actually did play the role of a fortified barrier. As we will see in the chapter on operational history, when Altan Khan attacked Beijing in 1550 he crossed the Great Wall through broken-down sections – evidence indeed that the intact wall was a genuine barrier – and in 1933 the Chinese Army held off the invading Japanese across the Great Wall at Xifengkou.

Whatever its actual defensive role, the Great Wall of the Ming dynasty was never the border of the empire. It was instead part of a deep defence system in communication with the capital via the web of signal towers that helped sustain it. The Great Wall was the 'front line' that followed a route chosen for sound strategic reasons, even if it owed its existence to political considerations. In this it was probably no different from any border walls or defence systems that had preceded it other than in the scale of its construction. A helpful analogy may be made with the Maginot Line. Like the Maginot Line, the Great Wall was supposedly a planned battlefield, with some forward positions, many linking

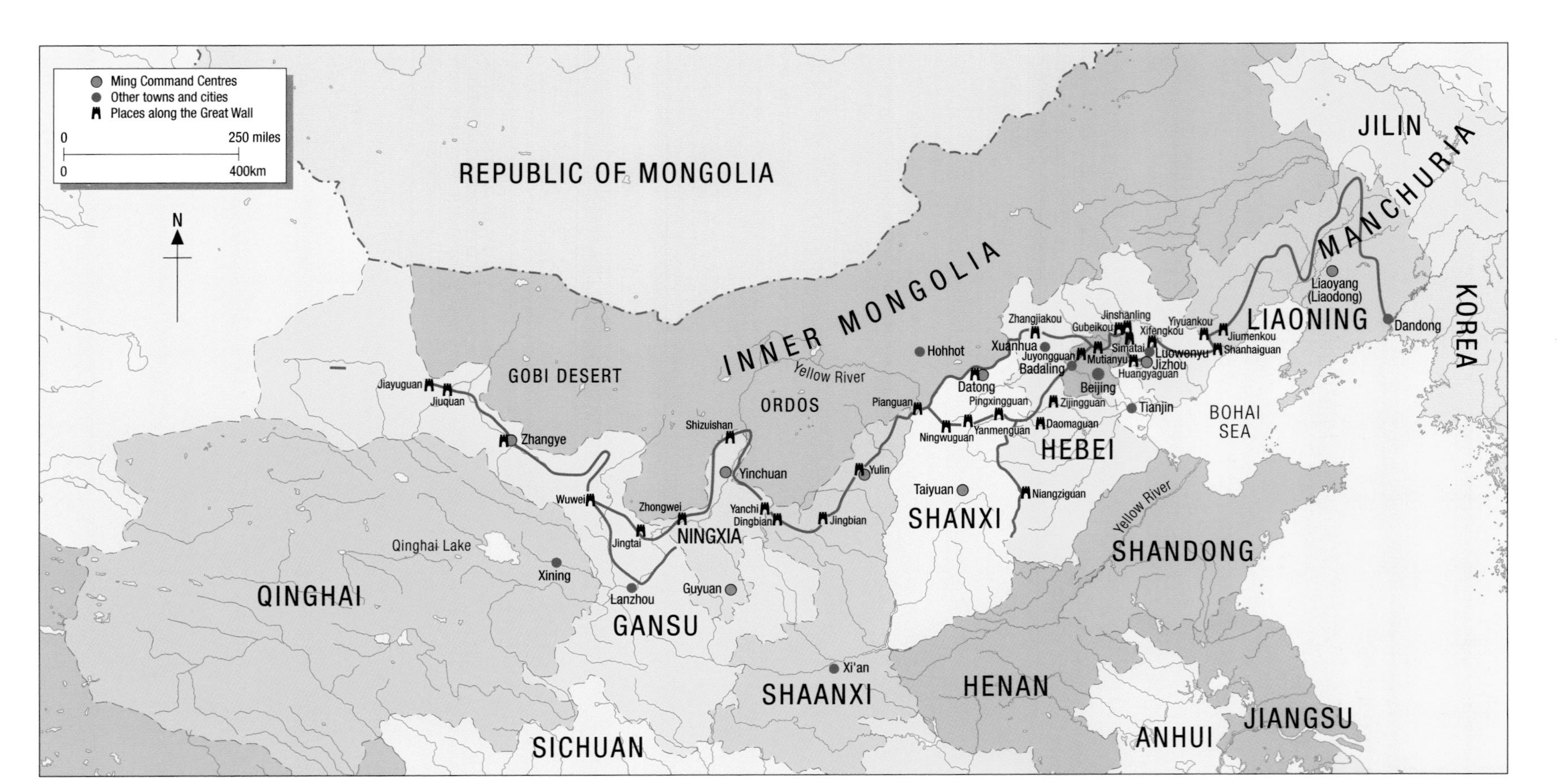


The Ming Great Wall, showing its location relative to the provinces of modern China; and the military garrisons or commands identified by the Ming as having responsibility for various sections. (© Copyright Osprey Publishing Ltd)

forts and towers to the rear, and considerable support mechanisms built into the 'front line'. Also, just like the Maginot Line, the Great Wall was tactically effective but strategically weak, and many decisions about it were made for purely political reasons. The Mongols could not hope to cross an intact Great Wall, but somehow they always found some way round it, while the Ming's Manchu conquerors were simply invited in through the front door. Gu Yanwu (1613–81) later commented 'it was not that the terrain was not precipitous, nor was the wall not tall enough; it was not that there were not enough soldiers or the grain was inadequate. The rule of the country, however, could not last long because the rulers had lost the heart of the people.' In the last resort, any defensive system is only as good as the political and military climate that sustains it.

The Great Wall occasionally hits a 'dead end' at a very steep slope or even a sheer cliff face, such as here at Huangyaguan. These were places where to build an easy link would prove to be as much to an attacker's advantage as it was to a defender's, so it was left undeveloped.

# The Great Wall at the operational level

## Defending the Great Wall

The strategic weakness of the Great Wall stood in marked contrast to its superb operational strength. At a battlefield level its formidable towers, rapidly traversable walkways and solid gates were virtually impregnable to a predominantly cavalry-based enemy. But the strength of the Great Wall as a defensive system depended upon much more than merely bricks and mortar, no matter how impressive their combination may have looked. Without the men to guard it the Great Wall was useless, but we must not therefore imagine that its walkways were constantly thronged by soldiers gazing northwards in the hope of spotting a Mongol raid. Less than a third of a guard's time would have been spent on military duties. Most of his day would have been spent working in the fields nearby; because one crucial aim of the Great Wall system was that its garrisons should be self-sufficient in food. The border settlers carried out farming, and higher-ranking soldiers were allowed to have their families with them.

This worn staircase on to the walkway at Mutianyu shows how much the Great Wall was used over the centuries.

Nevertheless, the deep depressions worn into the flights of steps that lead from the fields to the Great Wall's battlements show that considerable activity went on along the Wall. Much time would be spent bringing in supplies, cleaning and repairing weapons and tower maintenance. When defence was required bows, particularly crossbows, and later guns were used.

Spears, halberds and swords were the main edged weapons with which to repel a raiding party, while stones could be dropped from the apertures along the parapet. The *zhang qiang* (transverse walls) provided a useful series of defensive barriers if an enemy gained access to the walkway, and even if some towers might be lost, the strongest towers with their retractable rope ladders would provide a formidable barrier until reinforcements arrived. An elaborate variation on the rope ladder, although one apparently used only in the detached towers, was a wooden platform on which one man could stand, fastened by two long ropes to two winches which would be wound up to take him to safety.

A Ming dynasty 'recommended equipment list' for a five-man crew in an individual watchtower may not have differed much other than in scale for the garrison of a tower on the Great Wall. It lists a bedstead, a fireplace with a cauldron, one water jar, five cups and five saucers, rice, salted vegetables, three 'big guns', and finally wolf dung and a brazier for signalling, a vital duty to which we will now turn.

## Signalling and intelligence gathering

One of the most vital functions of the towers on the Great Wall was signalling, an importance underlined by the fact that whenever the idea of a long wall fell into abeyance individual beacon towers continued to be built and used. Some of the most abundant and valuable data for military life on the Great Wall may be obtained from the numerous references to signalling stations.

During the Han dynasty, when towers consisted of rammed earth, signals were not made from a brazier on top of a tower but by using a basket containing dry wood and grass. The basket was fastened to the end of a pivoted sweep up to about 10m long. As the sweep was mounted on top of a tower that may have been over 15m high the beacon could be swung high into the sky when raiders were spotted. At night it would be the flames given off that were recognized. By day adding wolf dung to the combustible mixture produced thick black smoke.

Contemporary documents describe the signalling towers as surrounded by their own defensive barriers, and including living quarters for the crews and stabling for their horses. The size of the crew depended upon the importance of the site. Those immediately adjacent to the Han Great Wall would have been well defended. Additional duties included operating a courier system (which had to replace signals in the case of fog), agricultural work and keeping records of observations and actions taken. Under the Han there were two types of signals required: a regular 'all clear' and a series of warning messages. Should the regular signal fail to appear, the crew of the next tower in the chain would investigate the matter. If the tower came under attack, two signals meant that the enemy numbered 20 men, three signals meant a raiding party of up to 100 men. It has been estimated that 10,000 men would have been needed to man the extensive network of Han beacons, watchtowers and sections of wall, let alone their reserves and support personnel.

Under the early Ming an even more elaborate system of signal towers was created. Liaodong, for example, had no less than 2,710 towers in all. A text by General Qi Jiguang mentions the use of wolf dung for smoke signals, but notes that it was difficult to obtain in the south, and as the account goes on to mention a black flag and a white flag, cannon and some lanterns we may presume that these items provided an alternative way of signalling.

One other vital function carried out from the security of the Great Wall and its towers was the gathering of intelligence. This could take the form of mounted patrols or the more hazardous method of spying deep within the Mongol territories. In 1449 some agents even penetrated the Mongol camps and carried out assassinations. In 1450 a group entered a Mongol camp and started fires in various locations just to let the Mongols know that the border was on the alert.

One of the most valuable functions of the towers on the Great Wall was signalling. Fire would be used by night. Black smoke, produced by adding wolf dung to the combustible mixture, was used during daylight. This illustration is in the Great Wall Museum at Huangyaguan.

## Artillery on the Great Wall

Various forms of cannon were mounted on the Ming Great Wall. The Mongols, it was said, were afraid of 'magical guns' – a somewhat optimistic statement in view of the Yuan dynasty's enthusiastic adoption of firearms. The Yuan were in fact the first rulers in the history of the world to make use of metal-barrelled cannon, which appeared in Chinese sieges decades before similar weapons were being employed in Europe. These primitive Chinese cannon were clearly valued as defensive siege weapons, because a Ming edict of 1412 ordered the stationing of batteries of five cannon at each of the frontier passes as a form of garrison artillery. Some designs of Chinese cannon saw very long service. For example the 'crouching tiger cannon', which dates from 1368, was still being used against

Defending a wall using crossbows and spears. This is not actually the Han dynasty Great Wall but the defeat of the 'terracotta' army of the Qin emperor by Xiang Yu in 207 BC. Nevertheless, we see similar weapons being used from behind similar rammed-earth walls.

the Japanese in Korea in 1592. It was fitted with a curious loose metal collar with two legs so that it needed no external carriage for laying. Another was the 'great general cannon', of which several sizes existed, and an account of 1606 notes a range of 800 paces. The enthusiastic description continues:

> A single shot has the power of thunderbolt, causing several hundred casualties among men and horses. If thousands, or tens of thousands, were placed in position along the frontiers, and every one of them manned by soldiers well trained to use them, then [we should be] invincible.

The curious *zhang qiang* (transverse walls) are unique to the Great Wall at Jinshanling. They extend halfway across the walkway and provided defences against a sudden occupation of a section of the wall by a raiding party.

A partially ruined section of the Great Wall lying beyond the much-visited Badaling section. (Photograph by Ian Clark)

From the early 16th century onwards a different type of cannon entered the Chinese arsenal, and this one came from Europe. It was known as the *folang zhi,* which means 'Frankish gun', 'the Franks' being a general term for any inhabitants of the lands to the west. Instead of being rammed down from the muzzle, ball, powder and wad were introduced into the breech inside a sturdy container shaped like a large tankard with a handle. A metal or wooden wedge was driven in behind it to make as tight a fit against the barrel opening as could reasonably be expected, and the gun was fired. The main disadvantage was leakage around the muzzle and a consequent loss of explosive energy, but this was compensated for by a comparatively high rate of fire, as several breech containers could be prepared in advance. The description of an early *folang zhi* notes that it weighed about 120kg. Its chambers, of which three were supplied for rotational use, weighed 18kg each, and fired a small lead shot of 300g. In 1530 it was proposed that *folang zhi* should be mounted in the towers of the Great Wall and in the communication towers.

By 1606 the breech-loading principle had been extended to larger-sized guns, and one called the 'invincible general', which was favoured by General Qi Jiguang, weighed 630kg, could fire grape shot over 60m and was mounted on a wheeled carriage. Another European cannon came China's way very early in the 17th century, when a huge gun, larger than any seen in China up to that time, was obtained from a visiting European ship. It was 6m long, and weighed 1,800kg. Because of its origin the weapon was christened the 'red (-haired) barbarian gun', and it was remarked that it could demolish any stone city wall. The Ming were so impressed that the Portuguese in Macao were invited to send artillery units north to Beijing to defend the capital against the Manchu threat, and the Jesuit priests who accompanied them were set to work in setting up a cannon foundry, which they did with some success.

A cannon emplacement on the Great Wall at Mutianyu with a reproduction iron cannon. Real cannon would not have been cemented into their carriages!

The Ming attributed their success in holding the Manchus at bay outside the Great Wall to their superiority in firearms of all sorts. In 1621 'the cannon were brought to the frontier of the empire, at the borders with the Tartars (Manchus) who having come with troops close to the Great Wall were so terrified by the damage they did when they were fired that they took to flight and no longer dared to come near again'. This was something of an exaggeration, but Nurhachi, the founder of the Qing dynasty, made great efforts to obtain guns of his own, and by 1640 it was reported that his successors had forged 60 cannon 'too heavy to carry round'. Other rebels against the Ming had firearms too, including Li Zicheng, who eventually overthrew the dynasty.

Looking down into the enclosed courtyard of the First Pass Under Heaven at Shanhaiguan we see the narrow tunnel that was so well guarded.

# The Great Wall from end to end

As the previous pages will have made clear, a historical survey of the Great Wall of China reveals that there are several 'great walls', not just one. Any attempt to 'join up' structures that were built centuries apart, and to project on to them some conscious decision by their designers to build, or even add to, a notional Great Wall that had lasted for 1,000 years, is totally to misinterpret the situation. This is a particularly important point to consider when describing the geography of the Great Wall, because each section has to be identified not only in terms of its location but also according to when it was built.

The description that follows can only be a brief summary of the main features along the immense Great Wall. A comprehensive list would require several entire books, and the photographs in Schwarz's *The Great Wall of China* (see page 63) will give the reader a good idea of the size of the task. This short gazetteer will look at the Great Wall from east to west, the conventional way of doing so. As the Ming Great Wall is the most prominent survivor of China's border defences, it is sensible to use it as a framework by referring to the 11 military garrisons or commands along the Great Wall. Nine were created at the time of the Ming dynasty's foundation, and two others were added when the capital was moved from Nanjing to Beijing. The border defences built at other times will be noted where they occur along the route.

The sequence of wall building under the Ming reflected the shifting locations of the current Mongol threat, which was in turn affected by the pressure placed on them by wall construction. Yu Zijun's successful Ordos wall of the 1470s naturally directed the nomads' attacks eastwards, and by the early 1500s the areas under most threat were the Datong and Xuanfu Commands, where no walls had then been built. As the fortified barrier grew, the Mongols moved round to the north-east and east of the capital where most of the building of the late Ming dynasty took place. Other lines of defence were maintained in Liaodong to the east and Gansu in the west. There were also inner and outer walls, spurs and detached sections in a bewildering pattern of construction and reconstruction.

The Xifengkou Pass, from an old photograph taken before this section of the Great Wall was submerged under the waters of the Panjiakou Reservoir. In 1933 the Chinese army held the invading Japanese at bay at this spot.

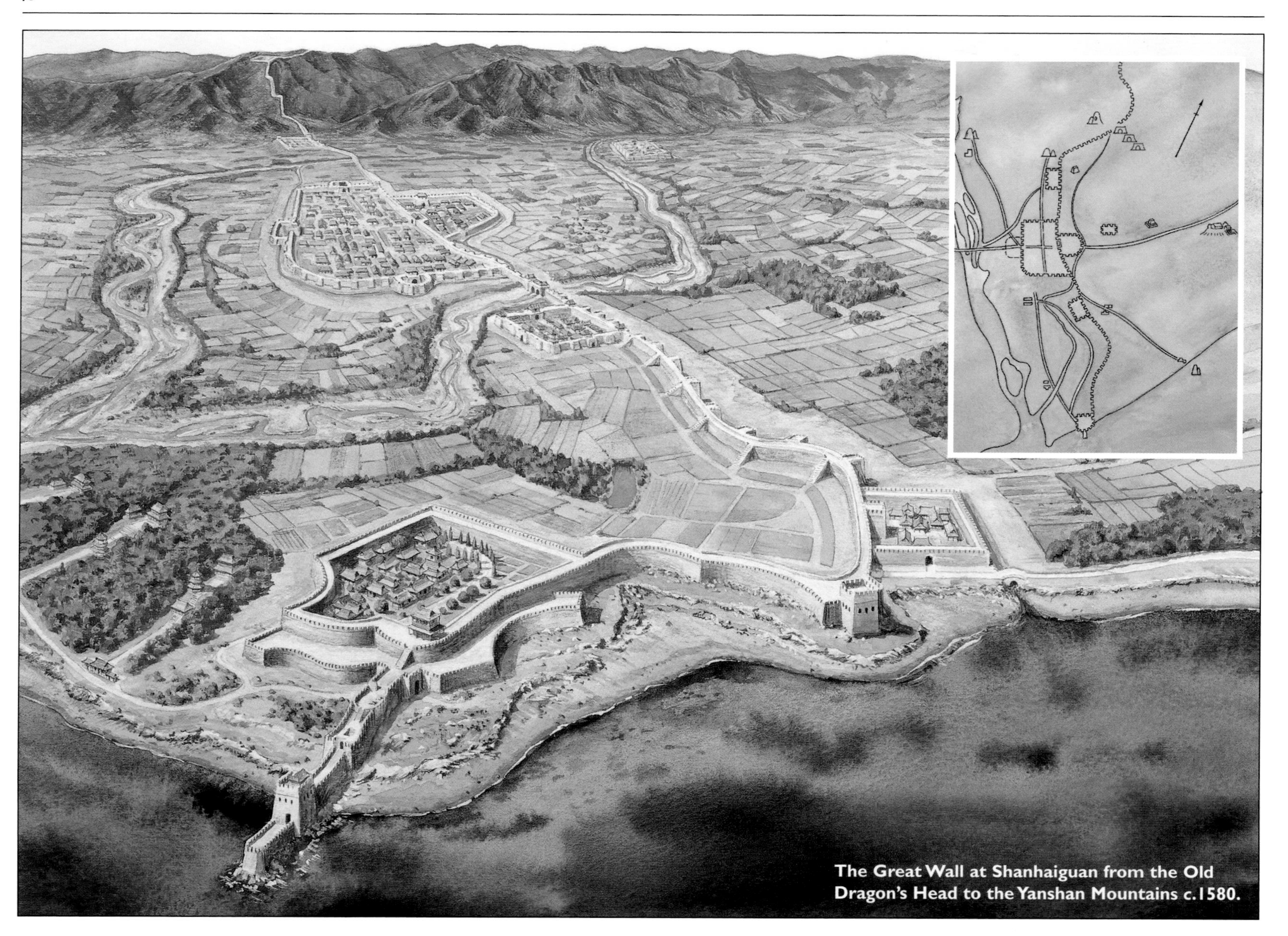

The Great Wall at Shanhaiguan from the Old Dragon's Head to the Yanshan Mountains c.1580.

Laolongtou (the Old Dragon's Head) projects into the sea. This recently rebuilt tower (the original was destroyed during the Boxer Rebellion) derives its name from the image of the dragon that is the Great Wall bending to drink from the sea.

The first problem is where to begin. Although the Great Wall has its 'official' eastern terminus at the Old Dragon's Head near Shanhaiguan an extension was built further east through Liaoning province to the Yalu River (now the border with North Korea) at Dandong. This section came under the jurisdiction of the Liaodong Command based at Liaoyang. Ancient walls are believed to have been constructed here before the Ming dynasty. The Ming wall consists of a variety of styles including rammed-earth and dry-stone sections with many separate watchtowers. There is also an important river crossing at Jiumenkou, where the Great Wall becomes a bridge.

The next section along – the Jizhou Command (later subdivided into Jizhou, Chang and Zhenbao) – which runs from the shore of the Bohai Sea to Juyongguan, includes some of the best-known portions of the Great Wall. It also contains its official beginning, which is to be found at Laolongtou (the Old Dragon's Head). This recently rebuilt tower (the original was destroyed during the Boxer Rebellion) projects into the sea, making the perfect eastern terminus for the Great Wall of China. Its name is derived from the image of the dragon that is the Great Wall bending to drink from the sea.

A short distance inland is the town of Shanhaiguan, which is built across the pass of the same name. The Northern Qi first fortified this very important area and the Ming walls were begun in 1382 under Xu Da. The Great Wall at Shanhaiguan is an impressive fortress complex built round the famous First Pass Under Heaven, a huge gatehouse complex protected by a courtyard. The Great Wall then begins its dramatic ascent of the Yanshan Mountains, reaching a height of 519m above sea level. Travelling west we encounter the Xifengkou section, where the defences were built by Xu Da, but the Luan River has now been dammed to form the Panjiakou Reservoir, so the Great Wall disappears

**The Great Wall at Shanhaiguan from the Old Dragon's Head to the Yanshan Mountains c.1580.**
This plate shows the Great Wall from the place where it touches the waves of the Bohai Sea to its first ascent of high ground. Laolongtou (the Old Dragon's Head) projects into the sea and a signalling tower sits on top of it. The barracks for the guards lie just inland behind the Calm Sea Tower. The Great Wall runs along the coast for a short distance then heads inland to cross the river, where a fort defends it. It then reaches the town of Shanhaiguan, which is an impressive fortress complex built round the famous First Pass Under Heaven, a huge gatehouse complex protected by a courtyard. Two outer walled sections protect the town to the east and west. After another castle the Great Wall then begins its dramatic ascent of the Yanshan Mountains.

Leaving Shanhaiguan, the Great Wall begins a dramatic ascent of the Yanshan Mountains at Jiaoshan, reaching a height of 519m above sea level.

into it to emerge on the far side. There is an interesting ruined section not far away at Luowenyu.

The next major pass is the 'yellow cliff' of Huangyaguan. This fine location takes its name from the near vertical cliff on the eastern side of the pass through which the Ju River flows. Qi Jiguang was once in command here, and his statue stands next to a section of the Ming wall that dates from 1567. Huangyaguan shows many interesting features of wall construction, including several spurs and an isolated watchtower called the Phoenix Tower that lies beyond the wall. There are also certain places where there is no wall at all, because to build anything would have helped an enemy. Instead the natural cliffs are integrated into the defence layout.

The next major route through the Great Wall is the strategic Gubeikou Pass, through which passes the road to the Qing emperors' summer palace at Chengde. Gubeikou is reached along the Great Wall by traversing two of its finest stretches: Simatai and Jinshanling. Simatai is noted for its dramatic narrow ridges where the Great Wall ascends at 70 degrees. Some towers are also very narrow because of the reduced space on which to build them, so that the whole section is something of a *tour de force*. Adjoining Simatai, and physically connected to it by a footbridge across the modern reservoir, is the stunningly undulating Jinshanling section, built after 1570 by Qi Jiguang. Towers of various sizes and shapes follow its switchback course. Some of them are among the finest examples of the towers designed by the famous general. On several sections of the battlements are three sets of loopholes for firing from standing, kneeling and prone positions. Here also we find the *zhang qiang* (transverse walls) that extend halfway across the walkway.

Moving further round to the north of Beijing we encounter Mutianyu. This is one of the most heavily restored sections of the Great Wall, but the work has been done exceptionally well. Its 22 watchtowers have been built at regular intervals and vary from being complex structures to simple beacons. Among these, the most famous is a virtual castle made up from three interconnected watchtowers. Away from the restored sections the wall makes several dramatic twists and turns. Unlike Huangyaguan, where cliffs were allowed to be part of the defences, the emphasis here is on providing an uninterrupted line of communication. This has produced in one place the very odd-looking 'ox-horn wall', where the wall goes up a mountain and then down again in a 'hairpin bend'.

A short distance further on and the Great Wall splits in two. On the Inner Great Wall, Juyongguan guards the most convenient pass through the mountains. Traces of the walls built by the Northern Wei and Northern Qi dynasties have been found nearby. As noted earlier, it was defended against the Mongols in 1211 and 1213. Xu Da established the first Ming defences there in 1368, but it was not until the national humiliation of the Tumu Incident that it became a first line of defence. The present wall at the site dates from the early 16th century. Mount Badaling, the most popular tourist site on the Great Wall today, and the one invariably chosen by visiting politicians for their photo-calls, lies just to the north of Juyongguan. Building took place there in 1539 and 1582. A diversion off the Inner Great Wall occurs just before Pingyingguan, where a long spur heads due south along the line of the Hebei/Shanxi border. There is one well-defended pass along this dead-end route called the Niangziguan (Princess's Pass).

The Xuanfu and Datong Commands had responsibility for the Outer Great Wall, which divides Shanxi province from the Inner Mongolia Autonomous Region. Some sections of very ancient pre-Ming walls have survived in Inner Mongolia, including the wall built by the state of Zhao in the Warring States Period. The extant section was built of compressed earth and is about 2m high.

A strong tower on the Great Wall at Mutianyu. This example has an upper storey with two levels of loopholes and merlons. There is a pitched roof and prominent drainage spouts.

It is one of the oldest relics of the Great Wall. A preserved section of the Qin Great Wall, constructed out of dry stonework, is to be found south of Hohhot. The Great Wall built under the Jurchen Jin dynasty dates to the 12th or 13th century. The Jurchen people had a different way of building their border defences. They began by digging a ditch and using the earth excavated from it to build an earthwork parapet.

Pingxingguan, Yanmenguan and Ningwuguan were vital passes along the Inner Great Wall that fell under the jurisdiction of the Taiyuan Command. Long before the Ming Great Wall was built General Yang Ye of the Song dynasty won an important victory in the Yanmenguan against the Kitans. In 1644 the rebel leader Li Zicheng won a victory at Ningwuguan.

The Inner and Outer Great Walls rejoin just before the pass of Pianguan, and the Yellow River, which forms the border between Shanxi province in the east and Shaanxi to the west, is soon crossed. Here Yu Xulin built his successful wall in 1474 to divide the Ordos plateau from the fertile loess land to the south and east within the broad loop of the Yellow River. In time this grew to be a double defence line under the Yansui Command based at Yulin, where there is also a prominent separate beacon tower called the Zhenbei (Pacify the North) Tower, the biggest along the Great Wall. Yulin was of great importance to the Ming.

Mount Badaling, the most popular tourist site on the Great Wall today and the one invariably chosen by visiting politicians for their photo-call, lies just to the north of Juyongguan. Building took place there in 1539 and 1582. (Photograph by Ian Clark)

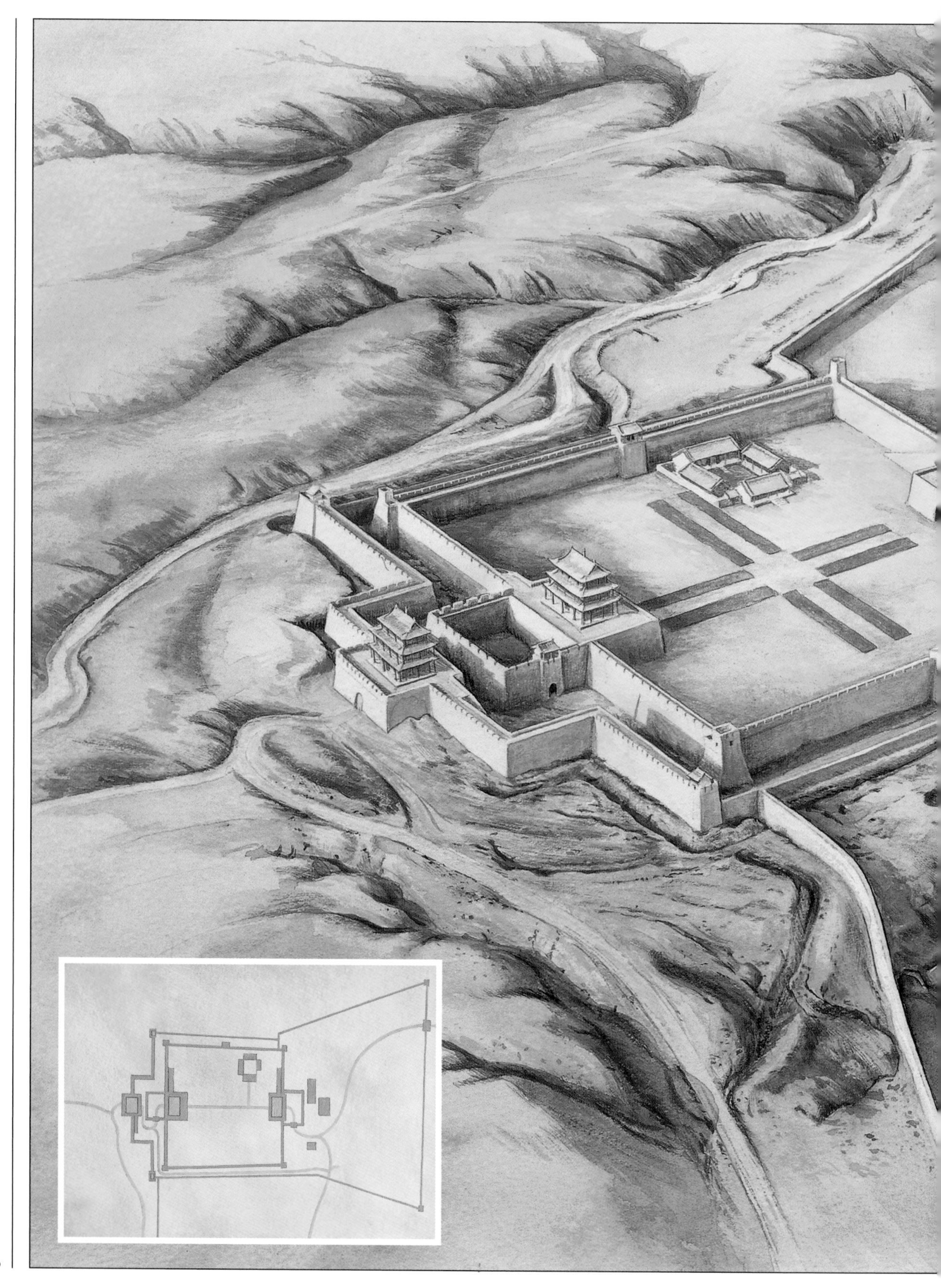

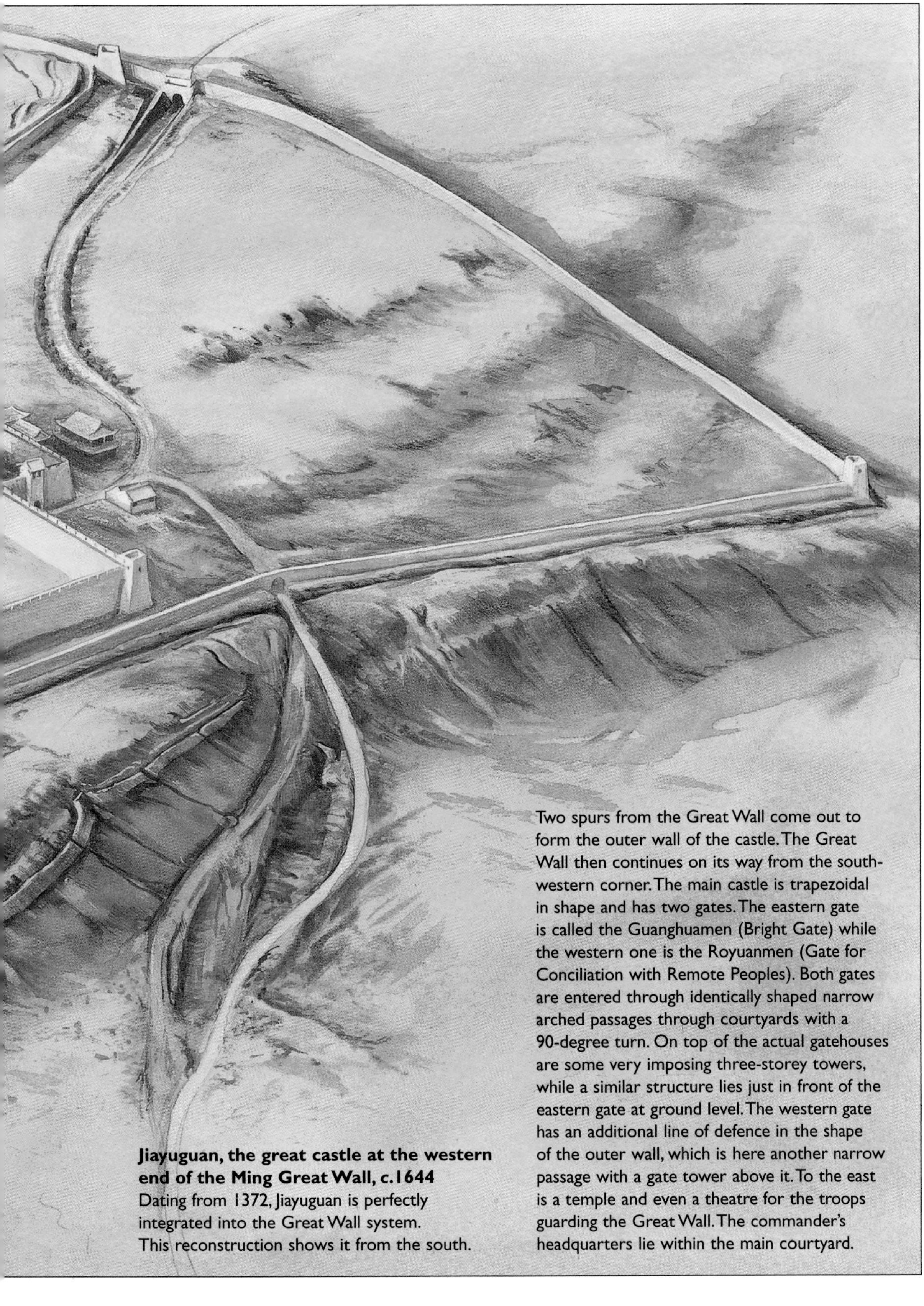

**Jiayuguan, the great castle at the western end of the Ming Great Wall, c.1644**
Dating from 1372, Jiayuguan is perfectly integrated into the Great Wall system. This reconstruction shows it from the south.

Two spurs from the Great Wall come out to form the outer wall of the castle. The Great Wall then continues on its way from the south-western corner. The main castle is trapezoidal in shape and has two gates. The eastern gate is called the Guanghuamen (Bright Gate) while the western one is the Royuanmen (Gate for Conciliation with Remote Peoples). Both gates are entered through identically shaped narrow arched passages through courtyards with a 90-degree turn. On top of the actual gatehouses are some very imposing three-storey towers, while a similar structure lies just in front of the eastern gate at ground level. The western gate has an additional line of defence in the shape of the outer wall, which is here another narrow passage with a gate tower above it. To the east is a temple and even a theatre for the troops guarding the Great Wall. The commander's headquarters lie within the main courtyard.

By 1403 it had become a fortified citadel and part of the Great Wall served also as one of the Yulin city walls.

The Ningxia and Guyuan Commands covered an intricate system of inner and outer defences through Ningxia province. With the turbulent Yellow River at its east and backed by mountains on the west, the Ningxia Great Wall, controlled from Yinchuan, provided a vital defence line within a tight bend. There is also a further line of defence to the south under the Guyuan Command, which rejoins the main Wall before Wuwei.

The so-called 'Hexi Corridor' through Gansu province is bordered on the north by the Gobi Desert and follows the ancient route of the Silk Road. The Gansu command was based at modern Zhangye, and covered the most westerly section of the Ming Great Wall. Its most prominent landmark lies near the Taolai River in the shape of the spectacular fortress of Jiayuguan. The actual end of the Ming Great Wall is to be found perched literally on top of a cliff overlooking the Taolai River in Gansu province. No more dramatic terminus can be imagined, but in fact the Great Wall of the Han dynasty continues at least 320km further west. This is the Yumenguan, or Jade Gate Pass, so called from the precious jade said to have been taken through it. The walls of the Jade Gate fortress and the Great Wall in its vicinity were built from rammed earth. It developed into a bustling market area, although by Ming times it had fallen into ruin.

But even this is not quite the end. Further west we find the marshy depression known as Lop Nur. It was once a lake, and its northern tip marks the very end of wall-building, although some beacon towers have been identified even further west and traces of a long wall may yet be discovered. It is now the area used by the Chinese as a nuclear test site, a strangely ironic touch for the final traces of the world's greatest defence project.

BELOW LEFT The *zhang qiang* (transverse walls) at Jinshanling provided a useful series of defensive barriers if an enemy gained access to the walkway.

BELOW RIGHT A view of the Simatai section of the Great Wall, from the point where it joins the Jinshanling section and soars up from the reservoir. The line of the Wall that extends from this point contains some of the most dramatic features along the structure's entire length.

# The living site

## Life and death on the Great Wall

During happy times when individual sections of the Great Wall were intact, maintained and unthreatened, the long barriers that channelled travellers in certain directions proved highly conducive towards trade, and from the time of the Han dynasty's westwards expansion the gates in the Great Wall provided a locus of security for merchants and traders alike. But that was when the individual walls were finished, and no time was more expensive in human lives than the years when the barriers were being built. 'One man died for every yard of the Great Wall' intones a popular work on the subject, which, although a hyperbole, sums up the enormous manpower resources that must have been required to built it and the sacrifice in lives that it entailed.

The harsh reality of Great Wall construction, whether under the Qin, Han, Northern Qi, Sui or Ming dynasties, was experienced by thousands of peasants whose livelihoods were directly threatened by the nomads. These luckless people were 'generously' exempted from taxes in return for years of backbreaking toil from which many died. In addition to carrying stones and bricks or ramming down earth, there were quarrying duties, timber cutting, trench digging, all carried out regardless of the burning sun or freezing cold and with the ever present risk of an attack by the nomads whom the barrier was meant to exclude. Nor was it only humans that suffered; quarrying and the stripping of forests and bushes degraded the whole environment near the Wall.

The Qin Emperor's massive civil engineering project left more than just folk memories of its appearance. There was also a lively folk tradition of the fate that befell many of the '300,000' men that Meng Tian is supposed to have taken with him. In fact the unfortunate general was indirectly one of the Wall's victims, because he committed suicide when Qin Shihuangdi died. His fate was actually ordered by the emperor's successor, who wanted a potential rival out of the way, but a colourful explanation tells us that he was full or remorse because in building the Great Wall he must have 'cut through the veins of the earth', and death was his punishment. As for his construction force, folk songs and tales about the building of the wall were current during the succeeding Han dynasty. One vivid example contains the words:

> If a son is born, mind you don't raise him!
> If a girl is born, feed her dried meat.
> Don't you just see beside the Long Wall?
> Dead men's skeletons prop each other up.

A fibreglass Chinese soldier mounts guard upon the Great Wall near the Old Dragon's Head.

The Calm Sea Tower overlooks the Old Dragon's Head where the Great Wall enters the sea. The original was destroyed during the Boxer Rebellion in 1900.

From poems such as these has grown the legend that the bodies of the dead workers were interred within the structure so that their bones would provide extra reinforcement. This has been disproved, but actual grave pits beside the Wall tell their own story, and it is a tale that persists in the popular legend of Meng Jiangnu. The story tells of a woman whose husband has been sent to a wall construction site in the far north. She is worried about how he will fare during the winter, so she sets out on a long journey to take him some warm clothes. When she arrives she discovers that her husband is already dead, and breaks down in tears. Her grief mysteriously causes the Great Wall to split open. The crack reveals her husband's bones, so she takes them back to his native village for a proper burial. Other legends spoke of a race of 'hairy men' whose ancestors had escaped conscription by Qin Shihuangdi and whose skin had turned white from living in the densely forested mountains for so many years. These 'hairy men' would ask strangers if the Great Wall was finished and whether the Qin Emperor was still alive. Unfavourable answers to either question caused them to flee.

## Guarding the Great Wall

The lack of winter clothing suffered by Meng Jiangnu's husband could also affect the crews manning the towers, whose daily lives were frequently miserable. In 1542 a note laments the plight of southerners sent north to man the northern frontier, where often eight out of the ten men crewing a tower died. This is almost certainly an exaggeration, but a high mortality rate among men who faced little military action must be attributed to a lack of food and clothing. In 1447 an order stated that fur coats should be supplied to the soldiers for the forthcoming winter. In 1465 padded coats, trousers and boots were issued to 4,400 men.

As for food supplies, in spite of the theoretical model of self-sufficiency through local settlements, food supply to the guards sometimes failed, even though the salaries of the crews were calculated in grain. Some crews received double pay as an incentive because of the particularly

Labourers build the Great Wall, carrying huge beams of timber and helping an ox cart full of stone on its way. From a bas-relief in the Great Wall Museum, Shanhaiguan.

dangerous nature of their postings. In 1453 many observation crews deserted their posts because of a lack of food. When raiding was likely the crews were unwilling to leave their posts to hunt for firewood or draw water, and even bribed the Mongols to leave them alone. In a classic application of bureaucratic reasoning, a subsequent truce with the Mongols in one area led the crews' commanding officer to cut their salaries because bribes would no longer be needed!

The accounts of daily life on the Wall and in the towers usually imply that the crews were drawn from the regular army. But on at least two occasions convicts were used. In 1470 in Shaanxi province, where the population was thinly scattered, it was recommended to use convicts to man the towers and ensure communications. In 1565 convicts were to be drafted to 'wall work', but maybe this means only as construction workers.

It is not therefore surprising to hear of crews under threat of attack either abandoning their posts or fraternizing with the enemy. The former behaviour will be discussed in a later section but the latter, which would be a serious matter during wartime, was normally encouraged during peacetime, because if trade with the Mongols was allowed there was usually peaceful traffic around the Great Wall. The nomads were often on friendly terms with the tower crews and sought to trade goods with them. This was to everyone's benefit provided it did not go too far and did not lead to the suspicion that the nomads were gathering intelligence for future raids. In 1453 some Mongols came to the Great Wall asking for mutton and wine and then behaved suspiciously by taking a close look at the observation towers. In 1552 an official noted that Mongols coming to the newly permitted horse fairs had torn down considerable sections of the Great Wall and destroyed many observation towers. The figure given was 'five to six tenths of the Great Wall' – an undoubted exaggeration, but one that caused real concern.

A long line of workmen carry stone up to the Great Wall, which is under scaffolding. From a bas-relief in the Great Wall Museum, Shanhaiguan.

On other occasions the crews were accused of laziness, timidity and negligence. Tribute missions from outside China sometimes chose to ignore official crossing points and passed through unauthorized sections of the Great Wall as they chose, but the tower crews on guard hardly gave them a second glance or even dared to question their purpose. Mongol espionage and opportunism were hardly necessary when situations like that prevailed. In 1550, just as Altan Khan was about to attack China, the military commander of Datong wrote:

> Our beacon crews and spies often go into Mongol territory to trade with them, and have made friends. The four chieftains ... have incorporated observation towers of our great border into their camps. The Mongols replace our beacon crews as lookouts while our soldiers replace their troops as herders, with the result that no strategic information on our defences can escape the Mongols.

# Operational history

## From boredom to battles

Peacetime life may have been uncomfortable enough, but when trade was suspended and the nomads embraced raiding once again the tensions along the frontier rose accordingly. There were a number of military skirmishes along the Ming Great Wall, although some of the most physically destructive 'attacks' it experienced came from the people it was meant to defend. In 1576 an official in Liaodong complained that the 'Lu' (i.e. the Manchus) and the 'frontier people' (i.e. the Chinese settlers) had been systematically breaking down border defences to steal building materials. Their targets included the Great Wall and also the signal towers, traditionally regarded as the 'eyes and ears' of the defence system, but often so poorly constructed that the crews no longer felt safe in them, and at the approach of an enemy they dared not raise the alarm. So numerous are the requests to repair individual towers and sections of the Wall that one is forced to conclude that there was either some shoddy workmanship and poor maintenance about, or frequent vandalism. In 1548 it was even suggested that old watchtowers should be torn down and the crews transferred to 'fighting towers' on the Great Wall; but for every report like this there is a contradictory report that praises the system.

Another scandal concerned the treatment of Mongols who wished to come over to the Chinese. In 1563 a report on corruption and treasonable behaviour among border troops mentioned that they had wantonly killed Mongols who had come to surrender, hoping thereby to receive some award for bravery in battle on the basis of a made-up story. Battle honours were clearly difficult to

BELOW LEFT The entrance to a tower on the Great Wall at Jinshanling, located next to a portal giving access on to the walkway, which is here made very narrow to accommodate the staircase.

BELOW RIGHT The bridge over the Ju River at Huangyaguan, which carries the Great Wall across the pass from the cliff face.

Mongol raiders attack the pass of Juyongguan c.1550

(PREVIOUS PAGE) **Mongol raiders attack the pass of Juyongguan c.1550**
Juyongguan was the most important pass leading to Beijing in the Inner Great Wall. From the time of the Tumu Incident in 1449 it was heavily fortified under the Ming dynasty. Like other passes, Juyongguan was defended by a courtyard requiring a 90-degree turn, but the outer courtyard of Juyongguan was a semicircle that surrounded the splendid gate tower that was directly connected to the Great Wall. In this plate some light Mongol raiders have arrived. They are the scouts for Altan Khan's advancing army. The Ming have cleverly allowed them into the courtyard and they are now being subjected to merciless arrow fire from the parapet above.

acquire, but any structure that was intended to guard a long, lonely and often nebulous frontier zone would inevitably experience an operational history that consisted of long periods of boredom interspersed by the sudden and sporadic arrival of danger.

In this the Great Wall and the isolated towers that complemented it as a defensive system suffered very similar experiences, because most actual fighting that occurred was on a very small scale. For example, sometime around 1500 the crew of one particularly flimsy tower provoked some Mongols, who took their revenge by tearing out a number of bricks and lighting a fire on the windward side so that the crew were suffocated. After an armed clash in 1553 one Chinese soldier fled towards a nearby observation tower and had to be pulled up to safety by a rope. In 1555 20 Mongols approached a tower and tried to climb it using grappling hooks, but just as one Mongol raider reached the top the snorting of their horses woke the tower guards. They bombarded the intruder with arrows and rocks so that he fell to his death and the others withdrew. On two occasions in 1539 the crews of separate towers were forced to fire 'resounding salvoes' to alert the army to come to their rescue. After another Mongol raid in 1553 the unfortunate crewmen involved felt 'isolated and helpless'. They lacked equipment and felt that they were being made to 'tackle dragons with their bare hands'. In contrast we have records of valour from 1547 when the sons of border soldiers who had died in battle were promoted in rank.

The tactical strength of the Ming Great Wall has already been alluded to, and this accounts for the paucity of records of any actual major fighting across its formidable ramparts. There is therefore an absence of operational history in this vein, which speaks of its success at a tactical level; but its overall strategic weakness is best illustrated by the major campaign of Altan Khan in 1550. His move against Beijing was enacted while the Ming were still embroiled in controversy about the correct policy to adopt towards the Mongols. In June 1548 Altan Khan's army had defeated a Chinese force, and on retiring successfully from yet another advance in 1549 the Mongols had shot an arrow into the Chinese camp stating that if trade was not allowed they would attack Beijing that autumn. But when the attack came the line of the Great Wall held, and no Mongol attack could penetrate it. Unfortunately, to reach the capital the Mongols only had to ride north, head towards the sea and strike south again, much as Genghis Khan had done in 1213.

In June 1550 Altan Khan passed through a broken section of the Great Wall in the Datong area and destroyed the armies that were sent to stop him. Later he joined up with new forces coming up from the Ordos. Faced again by another line of the Great Wall, the Mongols again diverted their route, and by September 1550 they were approaching Beijing along the route that led to Gubeikou. There they broke through the defences by sending cavalry detachments by minor roads and through breaks in the wall. Two days later they were encamped outside the suburbs of Beijing, which they looted and burned for three days. Their vanguard defiantly approached one of the city gates before withdrawing.

From the walls of Beijing a certain court official watched the nomads ravaging the surrounding countryside and wondered whether a particular column of smoke was rising from his own burning estate. Once the Mongols had left the retributions began. Some heads were removed from their shoulders, but the acrimonious debate rumbled on about whether to 'compromise' by granting trading rights to the Mongols or to take a further hard line. The political arguments resulted in the completion of the Great Wall system under the inspiring leadership of men like Qi Jiguang, but it was then almost too late. In 1616 the Manchu leader Nurhachi openly attacked the Ming and captured part of Liaodong. Following Nurhachi's death in battle in 1626 his son Abahai led expeditions against the Ming and broke through passes in the Great Wall on several occasions between 1629 and 1638 to threaten Beijing.

In April 1644 the rebel leader Li Zicheng breached the defences of Beijing and overthrew the Ming dynasty. The last Ming emperor hanged himself. Li Zicheng then marched east to confront Wu Sangui, the commander of Shanhaiguan, who represented his most immediate threat. Just outside the Great Wall were the Manchu armies. Wu was placed in a dilemma, which he solved by allying himself with the Manchus. The First Pass Under Heaven was opened to them, and they obligingly defeated Li Zicheng in battle. But that was the end of their services to the remnant of Ming power, and they rode on to occupy Beijing and proclaim the Qing dynasty.

## The Great Wall in modern warfare

Strangely enough, we have to wait until the 20th century to read of the next military operations involving the Great Wall. In 1900 foreign forces quelling the Boxer Rebellion destroyed part of the Old Dragon's Head where the Great Wall meets the sea. Shanhaiguan saw some fighting during the internal upheavals of the 1920s, while the second Sino-Japanese War of 1937–45 and the bloody struggles that preceded it from 1933 onwards saw the Great Wall playing the role for which it had originally been designed: as a physical barrier to battlefield-level warfare.

Following the establishment of the puppet state of Manchukuo (the name the Japanese gave to their possession of Manchuria) the Japanese planned to invade China itself, but across the most direct route to Beijing lay the curious physical barrier of the Great Wall of China. The Japanese attack concentrated on Shanhaiguan, which controlled a few kilometres of flat land between the mountains and the sea. Within the town was the gateway known as the First Pass Under Heaven. On 1 January 1933 a fierce attack by sea, land and air began. A Chinese army under He Zhuguo defended their historic position for three days before being defeated. Following this success, units of the Japanese army attacked other passes of the Great Wall in February and March 1933, but there the defences held, and the Japanese defeat at Xifengkou was regarded as a national humiliation. Equally strong resistance was mounted at Gubeikou, and the only way the Japanese were able to overcome the Chinese defence was by advancing from Shanhaiguan.

When the Chinese resisted the Japanese invaders in 1933 they used the ramparts of the Great Wall as a means of moving infantrymen rapidly from one sector to another, just as the Ming builders had planned. This photograph is of the battle at Xifengkou in 1933, where the Japanese advance was successfully stalled.

A Manchu attack on the Jinshanling section of the Great Wall c.1630

At Shanhaiguan there is also this very large corner tower, which forms an angle with the town walls. The original was built in 1587 and destroyed by Japanese artillery fire in 1933.

When the Chinese hit back they used the ramparts of the Great Wall as a means of moving infantrymen rapidly from one sector to another, just as the Ming builders had planned. Much fighting took place across the Great Wall at the major passes. In September 1937 the Chinese gained their first victory over the Japanese at Pingxingguan. The following month Japanese forces were ambushed as they made use of the pass at Yanmenguan, which was occupied by a Chinese force which then disrupted the Japanese communications. Fighting also took place at Niangziguan.

Shanhaiguan re-enters the story in 1945 after Japan had formally surrendered, when the remaining Japanese troops who were entrenched there refused to lay down their arms. On 30 August, supported by shellfire from the Soviet Union's Red Army, the Chinese under Zeng Kelin killed 3,000 Japanese soldiers in less than three hours, and the Chinese flag was hoisted above the First Pass Under Heaven for the first time in 12 years. But this was not the last that Shanhaiguan was to see of conflict, and three years later the red flag of the Chinese Communists was to be flown from the Great Wall when their army entered Shanhaiguan in triumph.

The events involving the Great Wall, which had played the defensive role allotted to it in a manner of which the Ming dynasty would have been proud, is remembered today in *The March of the Volunteers,* the national anthem of the People's Republic of China. The relevant words are 'With our very flesh and blood/Let us build a new Great Wall'. The song has had something of a chequered history that reflects the negative view of the Great Wall espoused by Chairman Mao Zedong. It was replaced during the Cultural Revolution by *The East is Red,* and reinstated following Mao's death in 1978 with different lyrics that mentioned Mao and the Communist Party. The original version was reintroduced in 1982. These developments, of course, take us from a consideration of the Great Wall as a military institution to its role as a national symbol, a vital topic to which we will now turn.

**A Manchu attack on the Jinshanling section of the Great Wall c.1630**
In this plate Manchu troops under the leadership of Nurhachi's son Abahai have forced their way on to the wall by using scaling ladders, in spite of the rocks, bullets and arrows poured down on to them. They have secured a length of the wall, but the Ming guards are mounting a fierce counterattack using the curious *zhang qiang* (transverse walls) unique to the Great Wall that extend halfway across the walkway.

# Aftermath: the Great Wall as a symbol

The Great Wall's symbolic role has been every bit as important in history as its military role, and there is insufficient space here to do justice to the topic. The Great Wall's popular image is a very powerful one. It is also a highly marketable commodity.

The symbolic role of the Great Wall begins centuries ago with the folk memories of the ancient Qin Great Wall and the hated emperor who built it. The folk tales about the death and suffering of its labourers have already been mentioned, and that awful memory was to result in the Wall of Qin being seen as a symbol of despotism, cruelty and ultimate political failure. When the Ming began to build walls of their own they took great care to distinguish their efforts from those of their cruel predecessors, but the similarity of the approach and the huge costs in human and financial terms was not lost on the succeeding Qing dynasty. Some of their scholars mocked the Ming for being no better than the ancient tyrant. By contrast the exemplary Tang dynasty had eschewed wall building in favour of a positive forward policy – just like the Qing, of course!

The knowledge that there was some sort of physical barrier in the distant country of China reached Europe quite early in its history and, with charming arrogance, it was naturally concluded that Europeans must have built it! The assumption was made that the wall of which travellers' tales told was the legendary barrier that Alexander the Great was supposed to have erected to confine Gog and Magog, who are first mentioned in the Book of Ezekiel (38, 1–6) in the Old Testament. The confining of Gog and Magog behind a barrier occurs in the Koran (Surah 18, 92–98) and Arab travellers were said to have seen the actual wall with which the story was to be associated.

From the 16th century onwards quite detailed descriptions of the Ming Great Wall are to be found in European writings. Maps soon augmented written descriptions, and the Great Wall appears on the map of China produced by John Speed in 1626. A mission led by Lord Macartney in 1793–94 appeared to confirm the grandeur of the edifice. Later visitors echoed his praise, culminating in the famous claim that the Great Wall of China could be seen from the Moon. This tedious piece of nonsense apparently originally derives from an article in *National Geographic* in 1923 and was taken up by a magazine called *Believe It Or Not* in 1932. The belief is still so firmly engrained that when China's first astronaut Yang Liwei truthfully reported in 2003 that he could not see the Great Wall his remarks aroused both disappointment and controversy.

The Chinese 'discovery' of their Wall happened much later than the Europeans' enthusiasm, and Sun Yat-sen, the republican who replaced the Qing dynasty, was the first politician to see the Great Wall as a potential national symbol. Mao wrote poems alluding to the Great Wall during the 'Long March', but his attitude changed, and during the Cultural Revolution hundreds of kilometres of the Great Wall were destroyed by quarrying and blasting, with the rubble used for road building. Local peasants were encouraged to help themselves to bricks to build their farmhouses. Deng Xiaoping's 1984 dictum, 'Let us love our China and restore our Great Wall!' is the creed that has replaced this destructive attitude. Tourism is now encouraged, thus producing a new type of pressure on the fabric of the Great Wall that may be even more destructive in the long run than the consequences of simple neglect.

# The Great Wall today

In 1778 the eminent lexicographer Dr Samuel Johnson urged his friend James Boswell to visit the Great Wall of China, because his children would then have a lustre reflected upon them from being the offspring of a man who had gone to view that unique edifice. It is a sentiment shared today by thousands of pathetic elderly gentlemen like the present author who embarrass their children by wearing T-shirts that proclaim 'I walked the Great Wall of China', even though the total length restored sufficiently to walk on is a mere 35km out of the 4,500km that remain. The rest is wilderness, not counting another 2,200km that have disappeared without trace, and it is a brave man who attempts to explore beyond the restored sections.

Nevertheless, a visit to the Great Wall is a uniquely exciting experience, and I cannot imagine anyone being disappointed. A guided tour is probably the best option for most visitors. Most trips to China take in a visit to the Great Wall, usually Badaling or Mutianyu, but walking tours visiting several different sections are also available. An interesting alternative is to join one of William Lindesay's 'Wild Wall Tours', which feature camping by the Great Wall or staying in other accommodation close by. In choosing a set tour the visitor should look very carefully at the itinerary provided. There will usually be one day in Beijing, which is well worth doing, but any tour that takes in Shanhaiguan, Huangyaguan, Jinshanling or Simatai will give a good mixture of

A tower looms out of the mist on the Great Wall at Mutianyu.

ABOVE The yellow cliff of Huangyaguan, seen from the Great Wall across the valley as the evening sun sets.

OPPOSITE PAGE The approximate locations of the surviving sections of the walls built by different Chinese dynasties that go to make up the structure known as the Great Wall of China. (© Copyright Osprey Publishing Ltd)

styles along the Ming Great Wall. I travelled on such a tour with the excellent Travelsphere, whose organization was superb and whose itinerary gave a great deal of wall for one's money.

With every year that passes travel in China gets easier and the Great Wall becomes more accessible, so any tourist advice in these pages will be out of date almost before it is printed. I will therefore confine myself to a brief survey of the most important sections of the Great Wall and suggest that the reader consults the latest editions of the *Rough Guide* or *Lonely Planet* volumes on China, or do an internet search to find the latest information on the accessibility of the more remote sections.

The Old Dragon's Head is very attractively situated on the coast. The barracks complex adjacent to it has been rebuilt and houses historical displays. Shanhaiguan combines city walls and the Great Wall in a fascinating ensemble. The First Pass Under Heaven is very impressive, and although its western side has been landscaped to within an inch of its life, it makes a dramatic contrast with the gloomy inner courtyard. There is a small museum within the gate tower, while the recently refurbished Great Wall Museum down the road is excellent and provides a fine introduction to the subject. The walk up to the Yanshan Mountains provides a superb view of the wall making its way to

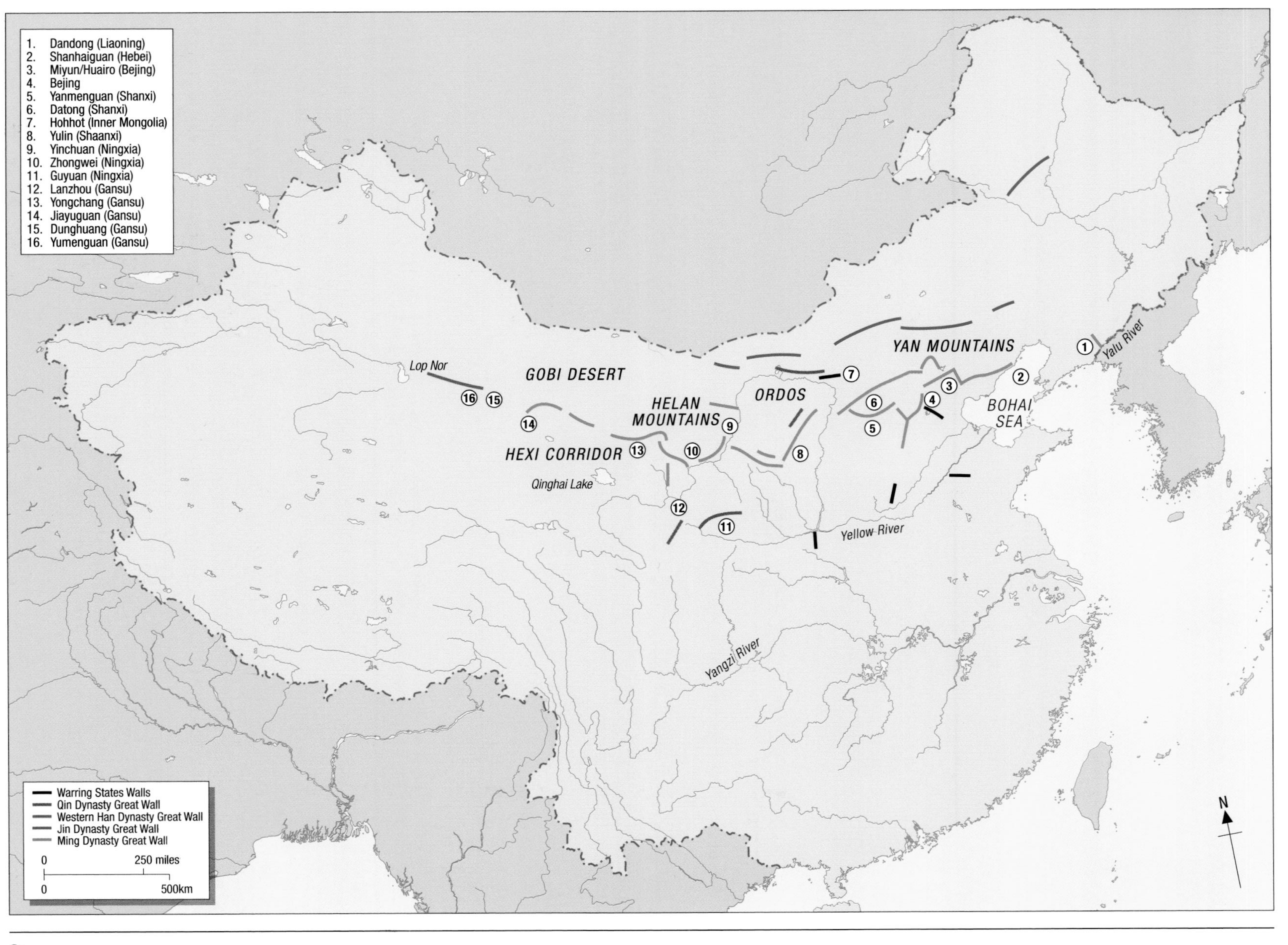
1. Dandong (Liaoning)
2. Shanhaiguan (Hebei)
3. Miyun/Huairo (Bejing)
4. Bejing
5. Yanmenguan (Shanxi)
6. Datong (Shanxi)
7. Hohhot (Inner Mongolia)
8. Yulin (Shaanxi)
9. Yinchuan (Ningxia)
10. Zhongwei (Ningxia)
11. Guyuan (Ningxia)
12. Lanzhou (Gansu)
13. Yongchang (Gansu)
14. Jiayuguan (Gansu)
15. Dunghuang (Gansu)
16. Yumenguan (Gansu)
YAN MOUNTAINS
Yalu River
BOHAI SEA
GOBI DESERT
Lop Nor
HELAN MOUNTAINS
ORDOS
HEXI CORRIDOR
Qinghai Lake
Yellow River
Yangzi River
Warring States Walls
Qin Dynasty Great Wall
Western Han Dynasty Great Wall
Jin Dynasty Great Wall
Ming Dynasty Great Wall
0
250 miles
0
500km
N

ABOVE LEFT The view looking down from the Jiaoshan section of the Great Wall towards the sea across the fields towards Shanhaiguan.

ABOVE RIGHT A channel for diverting rainwater and a hole for dropping rocks are seen here at Mutianyu. Note the slope of the brickwork

the sea. Some itineraries include a gimmicky boat trip across the Panjiakou Reservoir to see the edges of the submerged Xifengkou Great Wall.

Huangyaguan also makes an excellent visit. The wall soars up on either side of the pass and can be climbed with moderate effort. The Ming barracks have been restored and now house museums and a hotel: the perfect place to stay the night on the Great Wall itself. The Gubeikou, Simatai and Jinshanling sections are partly restored and provide the whole spectrum of Great Wall construction through their crumbling sections and broken towers that look like cutaway sections. Long hikes in either direction are possible. Mutianyu provides the finished product. All the restored brickwork is very neatly done, and the plain interiors of the various towers are very atmospheric. Mutianyu also has some of the most attractive landscape immediately around it. Badaling is the place most tourists visit if their holiday includes just one trip to the Great Wall and, although famously crowded, a short walk takes one away from the hordes. Juyongguan is not far away, and may be combined with a visit to Badaling.

The passes at Pingxingguan, Zijingguan and Niangziguan contain preserved features of Great Wall construction. Yanmenguan and Yulin are also of great interest, but are not of easy access to the independent traveller. Some tours incorporate Jiayuguan within a long Silk Road itinerary.

# Bibliography

There is a great shortage of scholarly work on the Great Wall of China. Arthur Waldron's essential *The Great Wall of China: From History to Myth* (Cambridge: 1990) covers its history very well, particularly on the political squabbles during the Ming dynasty, and I acknowledge the use I have made of it. His discussion on the Great Wall as myth is detailed and valuable but lacking in fieldwork observation. Nevertheless, interested readers should consult his work for the political history of the Great Wall that I have not covered here. Much information about life on the watchtowers, and by extension the Great Wall itself, is contained in an important article by Henry Serruys entitled 'Towers in the Northern Frontier Defenses of the Ming' in *Ming Studies* 14 (1982), pp. 9–77. Most of my references to local interaction between guards and Mongols comes from this work

Good background to the historical events may be found in the relevant volumes of *The Cambridge History of China*. There are also references to the Great Wall in David A. Graff *Medieval Chinese Warfare: 300–900* (London: 2002).

Any book on the subject by William Lindesay is worth reading, and his classic *Alone on the Great Wall* (London: 1989; paperback edition 1991) should be compulsory reading for anyone planning a visit, if only to realise how lucky we are today. He has also written *The Great Wall* (Hong Kong: 1999) and *The Great Wall: China's Historical Wonder and Mankind's Most Formidable Construction Project* (Hong Kong: Odyssey Guides, 2002). His small book *The Great Wall* in the 'Images of Asia' Series (Oxford: 2003) is an excellent one-volume guide to the Wall's history and construction.

For a remarkable visual tour of the Great Wall from end to end in high quality artistic black and white photographs see Daniel Schwarz *The Great Wall of China* (London: 2001). The weird and wonderful world of Chinese siege weaponry is covered in my two volumes on Siege Weapons of the Far East in the Osprey New Vanguard Series.

Several books in English have been published by the Chinese Great Wall expert Luo Zhewen, including the large format *Spanning the Ages: China's Immortal Dragon* by Luo Zhewen and others (Beijing: 1994). Luo Zhewen's *The Great Wall: History and Pictures* (Beijing: 1995) is effectively a shortened paperback edition. Recent years have also seen a growth in publication of Chinese books with multi-lingual text that chiefly consist of artistic photographs of the Great Wall. Some are remarkably good with beautiful and atmospheric compositions. Particularly fine artistic photographs by Li Shaobai appear in the beautifully designed *The Invisible Great Wall* (Beijing: 2004). In China I also purchased two popular tourist picture books both called *The Great Wall*, with excellent photographs. Each was excellent value for money and made a good souvenir. These are readily available, and actually cost less from the postcard sellers on top of the Great Wall than they did in my hotel!

# Index


Abahai 55, 57
Altan Khan 54–55
artillery 37–40, **39**

Beijing, Mongol attack on (1550) **53**, 54–55
Boxer Rebellion (1899–1900) 55
brick kilns **24**

crenellations **24**

defences 36–40
drainage spouts and channels **14**, 25, **62**

Esen 15

foundations **21**, 23–24, **23**

garrison life 36–37, 50–51
garrison towns 28, 29, **29**
gates and gatehouses **5**, 28–29, **29**, **40**, **46–47**
Genghis Khan 12
Great Wall
- construction 19–25, **22**, 49–50, **50–51**
- cross section **22**
- functions 32–40, 58
- gaps 33, **35**
- Han period 10–11, **13**, 37
- history 9–19
- maps **34**, **61**
- slopes **9**, 24, **25**
- switchbacks **32**
- visibility from Moon 58

Great Wall: sections
- Badaling **4**, **24**, 25, **39**, 44, **45**, 62
- Gubeikou 33, 44, 55, 62
- Hexi Corridor 48, 62
- Huangyaguan
  - barracks **29**
  - bridge over Ju River **52**
  - features 44
  - nowadays 62
  - spurs to Wall **26**
  - steps **16**
  - towers **25**, **28**
  - yellow cliff 33, **35**, **60**
- Inner Mongolia **20**, 44–45
- Jiaoshan **62**
- Jiayuguan 23, 29, **46–47**, 48
- Jinshanling
  - archways **29**
  - brickwork **11**, **19**, **21**
  - features 44
  - Manchu attack **56**
  - nowadays 62
  - slopes at **9**, **32**
  - towers **18**, **30–31**, **52**
  - transverse walls **38**, **48**
- Juyongguan 12, 44, **53**
- Laolongtou (Old Dragon's Head) **42–43**, 43, **49–50**, 55, 60
- Lop Nur 48
- Luowenyu **23**
- Mutianyu **15**, **24**, 25, **39**, 44, **45**, 59, 62
- Ningwuguan 45
- Ningxia 48
- Pingxingguan 45, 57, 62
- Shanhaiguan (First Pass Under Heaven)
  - drainage spouts **14**
  - features 43
  - gate-tower **5**, 29, **40**
  - military operations 55, 57
  - nowadays 60
  - towers **21**, 29, **57**
  - Wall around **42**, **62**
- Simatai 24, **25**, 33, 44, **48**, 62
- Xifengkou 33, **41**, 43–44, 55, **55**, 62
- Xinjiang **19**
- Yanmenguan 45, 57, 62
- Yanshan Mountains **42**, 43–44, **44**, 60–61
- Yulin 45–48, 62
- Yumenguan (Jade Gate Pass) 48

Great Wall Museum, Shanhaiguan **24**, **50–51**, 60
Gu Yanwu 35

Han dynasty 7, 10–11
- Han wall **13**, 37

holes *see* loopholes and holes
Hongwu Emperor 14–15

intelligence gathering 37

Japanese invasion of China (1933–45) 55–57
Johnson, Samuel 59
Jurchen Jin dynasty 6, 11–12, 45

Kangxi Emperor 18
Kitan Liao dynasty 6, 11
Kublai Khan 6

Li Zicheng 17, 40, 45, 55
loess 20
loopholes and holes **15**, 25, **62**

Manchus 6, 17–19, 40, 55, **56**
Mao Zedong 57, 58
materials 19–24
Meng Jiangnu 50
Meng Tian 9–10, **10**, 49
Ming dynasty 6, 14–18, 39–40
Mongols
- and artillery 37
- and the Ming 14–18, 41, 51, 52–55, **53**
- tactics 30–2
- Yuan dynasty 6, 12–14, 37

mortar 23

nomad raiders 4–7, **6**
- *see also* Mongols

Nurhachi 55

Ouyang Xiu 7

pavements **11**, 24–25
Polo, Marco 14

Qi Jiguang 17, **18**, 26, 37, 39, 44
Qin dynasty 9–10, 45, 49–50, 58
Qin Shihuangdi (Qin Emperor) 9–10, 49–50, 58
Qing dynasty 6, 17–19, 40, 55

*Shi Ji* 9–10
signalling **13**, 37, **37**
- *see also* towers: signalling

Song dynasty 11–12, 45
spurs **26**, 33
steps **16**, 25, **36**
Su Song 10

Tang dynasty 11
towers 25–28, 32, **59**
- corner **57**
- cutaway **27**
- entrances **52**
- functions 36–37
- interiors **18**, **30**
- larger **28**, **31**, **45**
- signalling **13**, 14, **25**, 28, 37

transverse walls (*zhang qiang*) 25, 36, **38**, **48**, **56**
Tumu Incident (1449) 15

walkways **15–16**, **24**, 25, **36**
walling types
- brick, stone and mortar **11**, 19, **19**, 21–24, **21**, **23**, **62**
- dry stone 19, **20**, 21
- rammed earth 19–21, **19–20**

Warring States Period 9, 44–45
water gates 28
weapons 36, **38**
Wei dynasty 6, 44
Wendi Emperor 11
Wu Sangui **17**, 18, 55
Wudi Emperor 7, 10

Xiongnu people 4–5, 6, 7, 10–11
Xu Da **12**, 14, 43

Yi Kaizhan 23
Ying Zheng *see* Qin Shihuangdi
Yongle Emperor 15
Yu Xulin 45
Yu Zijun 16
Yuan dynasty 6, 12–14, 37

*zhang qiang see* transverse walls
Zhengtong Emperor 15–16